Bergen Travel Guide 2025

Gateway to the Fjords, Seven Mountains And The Shimmering Norwegian Sea,Hiking trails and nature walks,Local markets and crafts.

Libby Martinez

All Rights Reserved Copyright ©2025. by Libby Martinez.

All rights reserved. No part of this book may be reproduced, distributed, or transmitted in any form or by any means, including photocopying, recording, or other electronic or mechanical methods, without the prior written permission of the publisher, except in the case of brief quotations embodied in critical reviews and certain other noncommercial uses permitted by copyright law.

This book is a work of nonfiction. While every effort has been made to ensure accuracy, the author and publisher assume no responsibility for errors, omissions, or contrary interpretation of the subject matter herein. The views expressed in this book are solely those of the author.

Trademarks: All trademarks, service marks, product names, and logos appearing in this book are the property of their respective owners. Use of them does not imply any affiliation with or endorsement by them.

VOL. 01

GALLERY

Table Of Content

Chapter 1. Introduction to Bergen — 7
- Overview of Bergen's charm and history — 7
- Welcome to Bergen — 8
- The History of Bergen — 9
- Why visit in 2025? — 10

Chapter 2. Planning Your Trip — 14
- Best times to visit — 14
- How to get to Bergen — 16
- Visa and travel requirements — 24

Chapter 3. Top Attractions in Bergen — 28
- Bryggen Wharf — 28
- Mount Fløyen and the Fløibanen Funicular — 31
- Bergenhus Fortress — 35
- Fantoft Stave Church — 38

Chapter 4. Exploring the Scenic Fjords — 42
- The Sognefjord: Norway's longest and deepest — 42
- Hardangerfjord: The Orchard of Norway — 46

Chapter 5. Must-Do Experiences — 53
- Hiking trails and nature walks — 53
- Seafood dining: Bergen's culinary highlights — 61
- Local markets and crafts — 63
- Northern Lights viewing tips — 66

Chapter 6. Family-Friendly Activities — 70
- Bergen Aquarium — 70
- Science Center VilVite — 71
- Kid-friendly fjord cruises — 74

Chapter 7. Accommodation Options — 77
- Luxury hotels — 77
- Budget-friendly stays — 78
- Unique stays: Cabins and countryside lodges — 80

Chapter 8. Getting Around Bergen — 82
- Public transportation tips — 82
- Renting bikes or cars — 84
- Walking tours — 87

Chapter 9. Day Trips and Nearby Adventures — 90
- Visiting Rosendal — 90
- Exploring Voss and its activities — 92
- Scenic railways: Bergen to Oslo — 96

Chapter 10.Insider Tips and Travel Hacks **99**
   Packing for Norwegian weather   99
   Budgeting your trip   104
Chapter 11.Closing Thoughts **107**
   Encouragement for your journey   107
   Bonus   107
   Travel Journal   110

Scan the QR code

1. **Open Camera:** Launch your smartphone's camera app.
2. **Position QR Code:** Place the QR code within the camera's viewfinder.
3. **Hold Steady:** Keep the device steady for the camera to focus.
4. **Wait for Scan:** Wait for the code to be recognized.
5. **Tap Notification:** Follow the prompt to access the content.

Chapter 1. Introduction to Bergen
Overview of Bergen's charm and history

Nestled between seven mountains and the shimmering Norwegian Sea, Bergen is a city that effortlessly blends natural beauty, rich history, and vibrant culture. Known as the "Gateway to the Fjords," this picturesque coastal city serves as the ideal starting point for exploring Norway's world-famous fjords. With its colorful wooden houses, cobblestone streets, and scenic harbor, Bergen offers visitors a quintessential Nordic experience.

Bergen's story dates back over 900 years, when it was founded in 1070 by King Olav Kyrre. It quickly became a vital trading hub during the Middle Ages as a member of the Hanseatic League, a powerful alliance of merchant guilds and market towns. Bryggen Wharf, now a UNESCO World Heritage Site, stands as a testament to Bergen's Hanseatic history, with its iconic timbered buildings preserving the essence of a bygone era.

Beyond its historic roots, Bergen is a city that thrives on creativity and culture. It is often referred to as Norway's cultural capital, hosting an array of music festivals, art exhibitions, and theater performances throughout the year. It was also the hometown of the world-renowned composer Edvard Grieg, whose legacy can be explored at his home, Troldhaugen.

Bergen's charm lies not only in its history but also in its seamless connection with nature. From its bustling fish market to the breathtaking views atop Mount Fløyen, the city invites you to embrace its maritime spirit and outdoor allure. Whether you're savoring freshly caught seafood, wandering through vibrant neighborhoods, or embarking on a fjord adventure, Bergen is a destination that promises to captivate your heart.

In 2025, Bergen continues to thrive as a modern yet authentic city, offering a perfect balance of old-world charm and contemporary Norwegian life. It's a place where every visitor can find something magical, whether it's the allure of its historic landmarks, the serenity of its surrounding landscapes, or the warmth of its welcoming locals.

Welcome to Bergen

Welcome to Bergen, a city that stole my heart the moment I set foot on its cobblestone streets. As I write this, I can vividly recall the crisp, salty air brushing against my face at the harbor, the smell of fresh seafood wafting from the market stalls, and the soft hum of a city that thrives on a perfect blend of history, culture, and nature. You've made an incredible choice by picking up this guide, and I want to thank you for trusting me to be your companion on this journey. With so many books out there, it's an honor that you chose this one, and I promise to make your Bergen adventure unforgettable.

The first time I arrived in Bergen, I was greeted by a sight that seemed straight out of a postcard: the colorful wooden houses of Bryggen Wharf, their facades leaning slightly with age yet bursting with charm. I wandered through the narrow alleyways between these historic buildings, feeling as though I had stepped back in time. The whispers of Bergen's Hanseatic past seemed to echo in every creak of the wooden floors and every shadow cast by the dim afternoon light.

One of my most cherished moments was taking the Fløibanen funicular to the top of Mount Fløyen. As the train ascended, the city below unfolded like a masterpiece, with its red-roofed buildings nestled between the fjords and mountains. At the summit, the view was nothing short of magical—a panorama that stretched from Bergen's bustling harbor to the endless blue of the fjords. I remember standing there, letting the wind tousle my hair, feeling both small and deeply connected to the grandeur of nature.

No visit to Bergen is complete without exploring its vibrant fish market. It was here that I had my first taste of Norwegian seafood: a freshly caught salmon sandwich that was both simple and extraordinary. The market buzzed with life, locals and visitors mingling as they sampled prawns, crabs, and even whale meat. It was a feast not just for the stomach but for the senses, with the sounds of cheerful banter, the bright displays of seafood, and the smell of the sea creating an experience I will never forget.

I also discovered the city's creative soul at Troldhaugen, the former home of Edvard Grieg, Norway's celebrated composer. Walking through the lush garden overlooking Lake Nordås, I could almost hear the melodies that Grieg composed here, inspired by the very landscapes I was now seeing. It felt like a deeply personal connection to Bergen's cultural heritage—a moment of reflection and wonder.

Bergen isn't just a destination; it's a feeling. It's the coziness of a café tucked away in a quiet corner of the city, where I sipped on a steaming cup of Norwegian coffee while the rain drizzled outside. It's the thrill of setting out on a fjord cruise, surrounded by towering cliffs and cascading waterfalls. It's the warmth of the locals, who always had a smile and a kind word, making me feel like I belonged.

This guide was crafted with love and attention to detail, inspired by my own journey and the countless wonders I uncovered in Bergen. I hope that as you explore this magical city, you'll create memories as vivid and heartwarming as mine. Thank you once again for choosing this book among many others. It's more than just a guide—it's an invitation to experience Bergen through the eyes of someone who fell deeply in love with its charm.

So, let's begin this adventure together. Bergen is waiting for you, and I can't wait to share its secrets and stories. Here's to an unforgettable journey in Norway's jewel by the fjords!

The History of Bergen

Bergen, often referred to as the "Gateway to the Fjords," is not only a city of breathtaking natural beauty but also a treasure trove of rich history and cultural significance. Its story spans more than nine centuries, and every street, building, and harbor whispers tales of its vibrant past. To truly appreciate Bergen, one must first delve into its fascinating history—a tale of kings, merchants, and maritime prowess.

Founding and Early Beginnings

Bergen was founded in 1070 AD by King Olav Kyrre, a monarch of the Viking Age known for his efforts to establish peace and prosperity. Originally named "Bjorgvin," meaning "the green meadow between the mountains," Bergen was strategically located on Norway's west coast, surrounded by seven majestic mountains and nestled by the fjords. Its position made it an ideal hub for trade and travel, setting the stage for its rise as one of Norway's most significant cities.

During its early years, Bergen flourished as a trading center, particularly in fish and agricultural goods. The rich fishing grounds off the coast of Norway supplied dried cod (stockfish), which became one of the country's most important exports. Bergen's harbor quickly became a bustling port, attracting merchants from across Europe and establishing the city as a critical node in regional commerce.

The Hanseatic Era: Bergen's Golden Age

The 13th century marked the beginning of Bergen's golden age, thanks to its membership in the Hanseatic League—a powerful confederation of merchant guilds and market towns that dominated trade in northern Europe. German merchants established themselves in Bergen, setting up shop in the iconic Bryggen Wharf, which remains one of the city's most famous landmarks today.

Bryggen became the center of Hanseatic trade, with its characteristic wooden buildings housing merchants, offices, and warehouses. Goods such as dried fish, grain, and textiles flowed through Bergen, making it a thriving international trade hub. Despite its prosperity, this period also saw its share of challenges, including strict Hanseatic regulations that prioritized the interests of German merchants over local Norwegians.

The Hanseatic League left an indelible mark on Bergen, not only economically but also culturally. German influence permeated the city's architecture, language, and traditions, shaping Bergen into a cosmopolitan city long before globalization became a modern phenomenon.

Bergen's Role as Norway's Capital

For much of the Middle Ages, Bergen held the title of Norway's capital, a testament to its importance in the kingdom. The city served as the seat of royal power, with Bergenhus Fortress standing as a symbol of its political and military significance. Built in the 13th century, the fortress remains one of the best-preserved medieval castles in Norway. It was during this period that Bergen became a center for Norwegian culture, governance, and religion.

Bergen retained its prominence even after Oslo became the official capital in 1299. It continued to serve as Norway's largest city for several centuries, maintaining its role as a cultural and economic powerhouse.

Fire and Rebuilding: A Resilient City

Bergen's history is also one of resilience. The city has been ravaged by fire multiple times, with significant fires in 1702, 1855, and other periods wiping out large sections of its wooden architecture. Each time,

Bergen rose from the ashes, rebuilding itself while preserving its historical character. The fires led to stricter building regulations, but Bryggen Wharf, with its unique wooden structures, was consistently restored, ensuring its survival as a symbol of Bergen's Hanseatic heritage.

The Industrial Era and Modernization

The 19th century brought industrialization and modernization to Bergen. The city's port remained a vital gateway for Norway's exports, particularly fish, timber, and later, oil. Advances in transportation, including the construction of the Bergen Railway (Bergensbanen) in 1909, further connected Bergen to the rest of Norway and Europe.

By the early 20th century, Bergen was a bustling, modern city with a thriving cultural scene. It became the birthplace of many Norwegian artists and musicians, most notably composer Edvard Grieg, whose works brought international attention to Norway's rich musical traditions.

Bergen in World War II

World War II was a dark chapter in Bergen's history. The city was occupied by Nazi Germany from 1940 to 1945, serving as a strategic location for German naval and military operations. Bergen suffered significant damage during the war, including bombings that destroyed parts of the city. Despite these hardships, the spirit of Bergen's people remained unbroken, and the city emerged from the war determined to rebuild.

UNESCO Recognition and the Preservation of Bryggen

In 1979, Bryggen Wharf was designated as a UNESCO World Heritage Site, cementing its status as one of the world's most important cultural landmarks. This recognition highlighted the need to preserve Bergen's unique history and architecture, ensuring that future generations could continue to experience the city's rich heritage.

Today, Bryggen stands as a living museum, housing shops, galleries, and museums that celebrate Bergen's Hanseatic legacy. Visitors can wander through its narrow alleyways and feel transported to a time when the city was the epicenter of European trade.

Bergen Today: A Modern City with Ancient Roots

Bergen has evolved into a vibrant, modern city while staying deeply connected to its history. Its bustling harbor, thriving arts scene, and innovative industries reflect a city that has embraced progress without forgetting its past. As Norway's second-largest city, Bergen is a cultural and economic hub, known for its music festivals, museums, and research institutions.

Yet, the essence of Bergen remains timeless. Whether strolling through the historic streets of Bryggen, exploring the majestic fjords, or enjoying the warmth of its people, one can feel the echoes of the city's 900-year-old story. Bergen's history is not just a tale of the past—it's a living legacy that continues to shape the city's identity and captivate all who visit.

In Bergen, history isn't confined to museums or textbooks. It's woven into the fabric of daily life, from the vibrant fish markets to the towering mountains that have watched over the city for centuries. To walk through Bergen is to step into a story that began long ago and continues to unfold, inviting every visitor to become a part of it.

Why visit in 2025?

Bergen, with its captivating blend of stunning natural landscapes, rich history, and vibrant cultural scene, has long been one of Norway's most beloved destinations. But 2025 promises to be a particularly exciting time to visit, with new experiences, enhanced accessibility, and an ever-growing emphasis on sustainability, all contributing to an unforgettable trip. Here's why Bergen should be at the top of your travel list in 2025.

A Thriving Cultural Scene

Bergen's cultural offerings are second to none. As Norway's cultural capital, the city is home to a thriving arts scene that includes everything from classical music to contemporary art. In 2025, you'll find more opportunities to experience the city's cultural richness, as Bergen continues to host world-class festivals, exhibitions, and performances.

- **Bergen International Festival (Bergenfest)**: One of Norway's largest cultural festivals, the Bergen International Festival will draw an even more impressive lineup of global artists and performers in 2025. With music, theater, dance, and visual arts filling venues across the city, this festival is a must for anyone interested in Norway's artistic pulse.
- **Edvard Grieg and Music**: As the birthplace of the iconic composer Edvard Grieg, Bergen remains a beacon for classical music lovers. In 2025, visitors can attend performances at the stunning Grieghallen concert hall or visit Grieg's former home, Troldhaugen, which offers both musical insights and beautiful views of Lake Nordås.
- **Modern Art and Museums**: Bergen is also a hotspot for contemporary art. The KODE Art Museums, which comprise several galleries throughout the city, are continuously updating their exhibitions, offering a fresh perspective on both Norwegian and international art scenes. In 2025, expect new installations and exhibits that explore the intersection of nature, technology, and human creativity.

Bergen's Accessibility and New Infrastructure
In 2025, getting to Bergen and exploring the city will be easier and more convenient than ever before.

- **Improved Air Travel**: Bergen's Flesland Airport continues to expand its international connections, making it even more accessible to travelers from across Europe and beyond. With more direct flights, it's now easier than ever to get to Bergen from major cities worldwide.
- **The New Bergen Light Rail**: The newly expanded Bergen Light Rail system, which is set to become fully operational by 2025, will make it even easier to navigate the city and its surrounding areas. Whether you're heading to the Bergenhus Fortress, the harbor, or the mountains, public transport in the city will be efficient, environmentally friendly, and easy to use.
- **Increased Ferry Routes**: Bergen is the gateway to Norway's famous fjords, and in 2025, the city will offer more ferry routes to explore these natural wonders. Whether you're traveling to the Sognefjord, Hardangerfjord, or further afield, there are more options to experience the awe-inspiring fjords in comfort and style.

The Rise of Sustainable Tourism
Sustainability is at the heart of Bergen's 2025 tourism offerings, with efforts to protect the environment and preserve the city's pristine landscapes continuing to grow.

- **Green City Initiatives**: Bergen has been consistently ranked as one of the most eco-friendly cities in Europe, and in 2025, its commitment to sustainability will be more evident than ever. Expect to see more green spaces, bike-friendly initiatives, and eco-conscious accommodation options throughout the city. Many hotels, restaurants, and attractions are adopting sustainable practices, from sourcing locally grown produce to using renewable energy sources.
- **Eco-Friendly Fjord Tours**: As more visitors flock to Bergen to witness the iconic fjords, sustainable tour operators are offering eco-friendly ways to explore these natural wonders. Electric-powered boats, carbon-neutral hiking tours, and green cruise options will allow you to experience the beauty of the fjords while minimizing your carbon footprint.
- **Protecting Nature**: Bergen's location in the heart of the fjord region makes it a prime base for exploring the wild landscapes of Norway, and in 2025, environmental conservation efforts will be in full swing. Expect to encounter more programs aimed at preserving local flora and fauna, including initiatives to protect Bergen's surrounding mountains, coastal areas, and forests.

The Stunning Natural Beauty of Bergen
Bergen has long been known for its jaw-dropping natural beauty, and in 2025, there will be more ways to enjoy it than ever before.

- **The Fjords and Hiking Trails**: The fjords surrounding Bergen are some of the most spectacular in the world, and 2025 promises new ways to explore them. Whether by boat, kayak, or on foot, the fjords are ready to be explored in all their glory. For those who prefer hiking, the mountains around Bergen offer an extensive network of trails, ranging from easy walks to challenging alpine routes. Popular hikes like Mount Fløyen and Mount Ulriken continue to attract visitors for their breathtaking panoramic views.
- **New Viewing Platforms**: In 2025, new scenic viewing platforms will open around the city, offering even more opportunities to soak in the magnificent views of the surrounding fjords and mountains. The recent addition of platforms along hiking trails and on the peaks of Bergen's surrounding mountains means you can now capture the perfect panoramic shot of the city in all its glory.
- **Wildlife Watching**: 2025 will also see a rise in wildlife watching opportunities, with more tours dedicated to spotting the rich variety of animals that call the region home. From seabirds to seals and even the possibility of spotting a whale, Bergen is a prime location for wildlife enthusiasts.

Bergen as a Culinary Destination
In addition to its historical and natural allure, Bergen has developed a burgeoning food scene, making it a destination for culinary travelers in 2025.

- **Fresh Seafood**: Bergen's Fish Market is an iconic spot where visitors can sample the freshest fish, from salmon to cod, and everything in between. In 2025, expect new gourmet dining experiences that put local ingredients at the forefront, particularly the city's renowned seafood.
- **Farm-to-Table Dining**: Sustainability is at the heart of Bergen's culinary revolution, with more restaurants embracing the farm-to-table concept. 2025 will see an increased focus on locally sourced ingredients, offering diners an authentic taste of Norwegian produce and culinary innovation.
- **Michelin-Star Restaurants**: Bergen's culinary scene is increasingly attracting global attention, and in 2025, visitors can expect to see new Michelin-starred establishments offering elevated dining experiences. These restaurants will showcase the very best of Norwegian cuisine, blending traditional flavors with contemporary techniques.

Year-Round Outdoor Adventures
Bergen's diverse outdoor offerings make it a year-round destination, and 2025 is set to enhance these opportunities.

- **Winter Sports**: Bergen is a great base for those looking to experience Norway's winter wonderland. With its proximity to ski resorts, snowboarding, and cross-country skiing, the city provides easy access to snowy adventures. In 2025, expect improved access to winter sports in the surrounding mountains, making Bergen a fantastic choice for winter travelers.
- **Summer Activities**: In the summer, Bergen's mild climate makes it the perfect base for outdoor adventures like hiking, cycling, and kayaking. The city's stunning parks, the nearby coastline, and the majestic fjords offer countless opportunities for exploration.

Unique and New Experiences
In 2025, visitors to Bergen can look forward to unique experiences that blend the city's history and modern innovations.

- **The Bergenhus Fortress Renovation**: The historic Bergenhus Fortress is undergoing extensive renovations, with new interactive exhibits and guided tours set to make the fortress even more engaging for visitors in 2025.

- **Cultural and Historical Walking Tours**: To further immerse yourself in Bergen's history, there will be an expansion of immersive walking tours that tell the stories of the city's past—from the Hanseatic League's influence to the Viking Age.

Bergen in 2025 offers a blend of the old and the new, the natural and the cultural, making it an ideal destination for anyone seeking adventure, history, and a taste of Norway's warm hospitality. Whether you're a first-time visitor or returning for another round of exploration, there's no better time than now to experience everything Bergen has to offer.

Chapter 2. Planning Your Trip

Best times to visit

Bergen, nestled on the west coast of Norway, is a city of unparalleled beauty, with its scenic fjords, charming wooden houses, and dramatic landscapes. However, the best time to visit can depend on your preferences and what you're hoping to experience. Whether you're after vibrant festivals, serene landscapes, or outdoor adventures, each season brings its own unique appeal. Below is a comprehensive guide to the best times to visit Bergen, complete with pros and cons to help you decide when to plan your trip.

Spring (March to May)

Pros:

- **Milder Weather**: Spring in Bergen brings a welcome thaw after the long winter months. While the weather can still be unpredictable, temperatures start to rise, and the city begins to bloom. You can expect average temperatures around 5-12°C (41-54°F), making it comfortable for outdoor exploration.
- **Fewer Tourists**: Spring is the shoulder season, which means there are fewer tourists compared to the summer months. This offers a more relaxed experience of the city's attractions, as you won't have to deal with crowded sights or long queues.
- **Beautiful Natural Beauty**: Bergen is known for its lush green landscapes, and spring is when everything begins to bloom. The surrounding fjords, parks, and mountains come to life, creating picturesque views of nature's rebirth. The cherry blossoms and colorful flowers make Bergen even more enchanting.
- **Lower Prices**: Hotels and flights tend to be cheaper in the spring compared to the peak summer months, giving you more opportunities for savings.

Cons:

- **Unpredictable Weather**: While the weather is generally milder, Bergen is known for its rain, and spring can still be quite wet. Be prepared for occasional showers and cool temperatures, especially in the early spring months.
- **Limited Activities**: Some of the outdoor activities, especially those related to winter sports, may no longer be available. Though hiking opportunities start to open up, you might miss out on the full range of outdoor winter sports in the mountains.

Summer (June to August)
Pros:

- **Ideal Weather for Outdoor Activities**: Summer in Bergen is undoubtedly the best time to enjoy outdoor adventures. With temperatures ranging from 14-20°C (57-68°F), the weather is at its warmest, and the days are long. Expect long daylight hours, with up to 18 hours of daylight in June, allowing plenty of time to explore the stunning fjords, hike the surrounding mountains, or take boat tours around the archipelago.
- **Festivals and Events**: Bergen comes alive in the summer months, with numerous festivals celebrating music, art, and local traditions. The **Bergen International Festival** in May and **Bergenfest** in June are two of the largest cultural festivals, attracting international performers and artists.
- **Full Access to Outdoor Activities**: All of Bergen's famous hikes, including trails to Mount Fløyen, Mount Ulriken, and around the fjords, are fully accessible during the summer months. You can also take advantage of boat tours, cycling routes, and enjoy the fjords' crystal-clear waters.
- **Vibrant Atmosphere**: Summer in Bergen is the peak of the tourist season, meaning the city is buzzing with life. The streets are filled with visitors and locals alike, creating an exciting, energetic atmosphere.

Cons:

- **High Tourist Volume**: Summer is the peak tourist season in Bergen, which means attractions, restaurants, and hotels can be crowded. The popular tourist spots, such as Bryggen and the Fish Market, can feel overcrowded at times, which may detract from the experience.
- **Higher Prices**: Since summer is the high season, you can expect prices for accommodations, flights, and tours to be higher. Booking in advance is essential to get the best deals.
- **Rainy Days**: Despite being summer, Bergen still experiences significant rainfall. The city is known for its rainy climate year-round, and while summer may offer warmer weather, you should still expect the occasional downpour.

Autumn (September to November)
Pros:

- **Pleasant Temperatures**: Autumn in Bergen brings cooler temperatures, ranging from 5-15°C (41-59°F). It's a comfortable time for exploring the city without the scorching summer heat. While the weather can get a bit chillier, the crisp air adds to the autumn charm.
- **Fewer Tourists**: As the tourist crowds thin out, autumn offers a quieter and more peaceful experience. Attractions are less crowded, and the streets feel more tranquil, giving you the chance to explore without feeling rushed.
- **Stunning Fall Foliage**: The natural beauty of Bergen is truly breathtaking in the fall. The surrounding forests, mountains, and parks are painted with shades of red, orange, and gold. This makes it a fantastic time for nature lovers and photographers to visit, as the landscape is at its most vibrant.
- **Lower Prices**: As autumn is considered the shoulder season, prices for accommodations and flights tend to be more affordable than in the summer months. You can still enjoy the city's beauty while saving money.

Cons:

- **Shorter Days**: As the days get shorter in autumn, you'll have less daylight to explore the city. By November, you may experience only 7-8 hours of daylight, which could limit the amount of time you can spend outside.
- **Increasing Rainfall**: Autumn marks the transition into Bergen's rainy season, and you can expect frequent showers. It's a good idea to pack accordingly with waterproof gear and a flexible itinerary to adapt to the wet weather.

Winter (December to February)
Pros:

- **Magical Winter Wonderland**: Bergen transforms into a charming winter wonderland during the colder months. The snow-capped mountains, cozy Christmas markets, and the twinkling lights throughout the city create a picturesque, festive atmosphere. If you love the winter season, this is the time to visit.
- **Christmas Markets**: Bergen's famous Christmas Market, held at the Bryggen Wharf, is a must-see. The market is filled with local handicrafts, food, and festive decorations, offering a truly magical experience.
- **Fewer Tourists**: Winter is the off-season in Bergen, meaning you can enjoy the city's top attractions without the crowds. You'll have more space to enjoy the famous Bryggen Wharf, the Bergenhus Fortress, and other landmarks without the hustle and bustle of tourists.
- **Great for Winter Sports**: Bergen's nearby mountains provide access to winter sports like skiing, snowboarding, and cross-country skiing. The winter months are perfect for those looking to embrace the snow-covered landscape.

Cons:

- **Cold and Short Days**: Winter in Bergen can be very cold, with temperatures averaging between -1°C and 4°C (30°F to 39°F). Snowfall can make travel conditions tricky, and the city's days are at their shortest, with only 6 hours of daylight in December. This limits the time you have to explore the city and its surroundings.
- **Limited Outdoor Activities**: While winter is perfect for winter sports, some of Bergen's famous hiking trails are inaccessible due to snow and ice. Fjord cruises may also be less frequent or altered due to weather conditions.
- **Increased Rain and Wind**: Bergen's notorious rainfall intensifies during the winter, often accompanied by strong winds. You'll need to prepare for wet conditions if you're visiting during this time.

When Should You Visit Bergen?

- **Best for Mild Weather and Fewer Crowds**: Spring (March to May) offers a balance of mild weather, fewer tourists, and beautiful blooming landscapes. If you prefer a quieter experience with lower costs, spring is ideal.
- **Best for Outdoor Activities and Festivals**: Summer (June to August) is the best time for exploring Bergen's natural beauty and enjoying its lively festivals, but be prepared for high tourist traffic and higher prices.
- **Best for Fall Colors and Peaceful Exploration**: Autumn (September to November) is perfect for those seeking stunning landscapes, fewer crowds, and pleasant temperatures, but the days are shorter, and rain becomes more frequent.
- **Best for Winter Magic and Christmas Charm**: Winter (December to February) is ideal if you enjoy snowy landscapes and festive Christmas markets, but expect cold weather, shorter days, and increased rainfall.

Ultimately, the best time to visit Bergen depends on your personal preferences for weather, activities, and crowds. No matter when you choose to visit, Bergen's charm and beauty will undoubtedly leave a lasting impression.

How to get to Bergen

Bergen, the second-largest city in Norway, is a popular destination for travelers seeking to explore its breathtaking fjords, rich history, and vibrant culture. The city is well-connected by air, offering convenient flight options for both domestic and international travelers. Whether you're flying from a nearby European hub or arriving from farther afield, getting to Bergen by air is a smooth and efficient experience. Here's an exhaustive and descriptive guide to help you navigate the journey to Bergen's airport and ensure a seamless travel experience.

Bergen Airport (Bergen Lufthavn, Flesland)

The main gateway to the city of Bergen is **Bergen Airport, Flesland (BGO)**, located approximately 18 kilometers (11 miles) south of the city center. The airport is Norway's second-largest international airport after Oslo Gardermoen, handling both domestic and international flights. Opened in 1955 and continuously expanding, the airport offers modern facilities, including a variety of shops, restaurants, and comfortable lounges, ensuring a pleasant experience for all travelers.

Airport Facilities:

- **Airlines and Destinations**: Bergen Airport serves numerous airlines and destinations, including flights within Norway, Europe, and a few long-haul options. It is particularly well-served by Scandinavian Airlines (SAS), Norwegian Air Shuttle, and Widerøe.
- **Transportation**: Once you land, you'll find efficient transportation options to the city, including taxis, buses, and the Flybussen (Airport Express Coach), which offers direct service to key locations in Bergen.
- **Shopping and Dining**: Bergen Airport features a variety of shops selling Norwegian souvenirs, electronics, fashion, and more. You'll also find plenty of restaurants and cafes offering Norwegian delicacies, international fast food, and premium dining options.
- **Lounge Access**: For those flying business class or with a lounge membership, there are lounge areas where you can relax, enjoy refreshments, and access Wi-Fi before your flight or upon arrival.

International Flights to Bergen
From Europe:

Bergen is well-connected to major European cities, making it relatively easy to reach from across the continent. Many international travelers opt for flights from cities such as London, Copenhagen, Amsterdam, and Frankfurt. Several airlines provide regular connections to Bergen, ensuring a smooth transition from Europe to this beautiful city.

- **London**: There are direct flights from London to Bergen, with flight times typically around 2 hours. Airlines such as **Norwegian Air Shuttle**, **SAS**, and **Widerøe** operate frequent flights to Bergen from London's major airports (Heathrow, Gatwick, or Stansted).
- **Copenhagen**: Copenhagen is another major European hub with direct flights to Bergen. The flight time from Copenhagen to Bergen is around 1 hour and 15 minutes. **SAS** and **Norwegian** are among the airlines that offer daily connections between the two cities.
- **Amsterdam**: With flights taking about 1 hour and 45 minutes, **KLM** and **SAS** provide direct service from Amsterdam Schiphol to Bergen.
- **Frankfurt**: If you're traveling from Germany, Frankfurt offers direct connections to Bergen with flight times of approximately 1 hour and 45 minutes. Airlines such as **Lufthansa** and **SAS** offer services on this route.

From the United States:

While Bergen does not have direct flights from the United States, you can easily connect to Bergen via major European cities like London, Copenhagen, or Amsterdam. Popular American gateways to Bergen include New York, Chicago, and Los Angeles. Many travelers choose to book a flight to a European hub and then connect with a short-haul flight to Bergen.

- **New York to Bergen**: The flight from New York (JFK or Newark) to Bergen typically involves a layover in a European city such as London or Copenhagen. After the layover, a quick connection will get you to Bergen in approximately 2 hours from your European stop.
- **Chicago to Bergen**: From Chicago O'Hare International Airport (ORD), travelers usually need to fly to an intermediate hub such as Copenhagen or London and take a connecting flight to Bergen.
- **Los Angeles to Bergen**: If you're traveling from Los Angeles (LAX), there are no direct flights to Bergen. However, a layover in one of the major European cities, followed by a short connecting flight, will get you to Bergen within 12-14 hours, depending on the layover duration.

From Other International Locations:

- **Dubai**: Travelers flying from the Middle East can connect to Bergen with layovers in European cities such as Copenhagen, Frankfurt, or London. Emirates, Lufthansa, and SAS often operate these routes, with an approximate total travel time of 9-11 hours.

- **Asia**: If you're coming from Asia (e.g., Tokyo, Beijing, or Singapore), you'll likely need to transit through European hubs like Copenhagen, Frankfurt, or Amsterdam. Expect total travel times ranging from 12 to 15 hours depending on the layover and connecting flights.

Domestic Flights to Bergen

If you're already in Norway, getting to Bergen is quick and convenient, with several domestic flight options available from major cities like Oslo, Stavanger, Trondheim, and Tromsø.

- **Oslo to Bergen**: Oslo is the main entry point for international travelers arriving in Norway, and from here, it's only a short 50-minute flight to Bergen. Several flights are available daily, operated by **SAS**, **Norwegian**, and **Widerøe**.
- **Stavanger to Bergen**: The flight from Stavanger to Bergen takes about 35 minutes. It's a frequent route, with flights provided by **SAS** and **Norwegian**.
- **Trondheim to Bergen**: From Trondheim, it takes approximately 1 hour and 10 minutes to fly to Bergen. This route is served by **SAS** and **Widerøe**.
- **Tromsø to Bergen**: For those heading to Bergen from the far north of Norway, the flight from Tromsø takes about 2 hours. **SAS** provides this route.

Domestic flights in Norway are efficient and well-coordinated, making it easy to travel between cities.

Connecting Flights and Layovers

If your flight to Bergen involves a layover in another city, consider the following tips to make your connection as smooth as possible:

- **Layovers in Oslo (OSL)**: Many international travelers will pass through **Oslo Gardermoen Airport (OSL)**, Norway's largest airport. The airport is well-organized, and the connection from international to domestic flights is seamless. A transfer to Bergen from Oslo is frequent, with multiple flights available each day.
- **Layovers in Copenhagen (CPH)**: Copenhagen is a major hub for flights to Bergen, and if you're connecting here, the airport offers efficient services for travelers. It's a small airport, so transferring between gates is quick. With direct flights from Copenhagen to Bergen, the layover will usually last only 1-2 hours.
- **Layovers in Frankfurt (FRA)**: If you're connecting through Frankfurt, you'll be passing through one of Europe's busiest airports. Be prepared for a bit of walking between terminals, but the airport offers excellent signage, so it's easy to navigate. Make sure to check if you need to go through customs before boarding your flight to Bergen.

Air Travel Tips for Bergen

- **Booking Your Flight**: Always book your flight in advance, especially if you're traveling during peak seasons like summer. This ensures you get the best rates and secure your seat on a flight that matches your preferred schedule.
- **Weather Considerations**: Bergen is known for its rainy weather. While the airport is well-equipped to handle inclement weather, flights may occasionally be delayed or rerouted due to heavy rain or fog. Always check the weather forecast before your flight and pack accordingly.
- **Baggage**: If you're traveling during the winter months, especially for outdoor activities like skiing or hiking, ensure you're aware of your airline's baggage policies for carrying sports equipment.
- **Arrival in Bergen**: Upon arrival at Bergen Airport, you'll find several transport options to get to the city center. The **Flybussen** (Airport Express Coach) is one of the most popular and cost-effective ways to reach the city, with a travel time of about 30 minutes. Taxis are available outside the terminal, but they tend to be pricier, especially for solo travelers.

Flying to Bergen is a straightforward and enjoyable experience, whether you're traveling from within Norway or from international destinations. With its efficient airport, well-connected flight routes, and ample transport options from the airport to the city, getting to Bergen by air is the ideal way to start your Norwegian adventure. By booking your flight in advance and considering the time of year and your specific travel needs, you can ensure that your journey to this beautiful city will be as smooth and memorable as the destination itself.

How to Get to Bergen by Train

Bergen, Norway's picturesque gateway to the fjords, is renowned not only for its stunning landscapes but also for its exceptional train travel options. Taking the train to Bergen is an incredibly scenic and relaxing way to begin your adventure, as the journey through the Norwegian countryside is a sight to behold. Whether you're traveling from Oslo, Stavanger, or other locations, the train ride offers one of the most beautiful and comfortable methods to arrive in this vibrant city. Here's an exhaustive guide to getting to Bergen by train, with all the information you'll need to enjoy a smooth and scenic ride.

The Bergen Railway (Bergensbanen)

The **Bergen Railway (Bergensbanen)** is one of the most famous and scenic train routes in the world, offering travelers a spectacular journey between Oslo and Bergen. Stretching over 500 kilometers (310 miles), the Bergen Railway connects Oslo, the capital of Norway, with Bergen on the country's western coast. The train journey is renowned for its stunning views, crossing the mountains and passing through some of Norway's most breathtaking natural landscapes.

Key Features of the Bergen Railway:

- **Route Length**: The Bergen Railway runs from **Oslo Central Station (Oslo S)** to **Bergen Station**, with the total journey taking about **6.5 to 7 hours**.
- **Service Providers**: The train service is operated by **Vy**, Norway's largest train company, which provides modern, comfortable trains equipped with amenities to enhance your journey. Trains run year-round, with multiple departures daily.
- **Scenic Views**: The train ride takes you through diverse landscapes, from lush forests and sparkling lakes to dramatic mountains and deep valleys. The section between **Finse** and **Myrdal** is particularly popular for its views of snow-capped peaks, alpine lakes, and vast stretches of wilderness. Keep your camera handy because the vistas are truly unforgettable.

Departing from Oslo to Bergen: The Journey Overview

The **Oslo to Bergen** train journey begins at **Oslo Central Station (Oslo S)**, a bustling transport hub in the heart of Norway's capital. From here, you'll board the Bergen Railway for the picturesque trip across the mountains to Bergen.

Route Overview:

- **Oslo to Geilo**: The journey begins by heading out of Oslo, passing through forests and lakes, and climbing into the mountainous terrain. After about 2.5 hours, the train will stop at **Geilo**, a popular ski resort located in the Hallingdal Valley. This area is known for its stunning natural beauty and winter sports, offering travelers a brief glimpse of Norway's alpine landscape.
- **Geilo to Finse**: Continuing on, the train moves further into the highlands, passing through **Finse**, Norway's highest railway station, at 1,222 meters (4,040 feet) above sea level. This part of the journey takes you through stark, snow-covered landscapes, even in the summer months. It's an iconic part of the route and is especially famous for the "wild" natural beauty of the area.
- **Myrdal and the Flåm Railway**: The train stops at **Myrdal**, a small station that connects to the famous **Flåm Railway**, a must-do excursion if you want to explore the Aurlandsfjord. This steep and narrow railway takes you down into the scenic village of **Flåm**, nestled at the bottom of the fjord. Although this side trip is optional, it's highly recommended for a more immersive fjord experience.
- **Myrdal to Bergen**: As the train continues from Myrdal, the landscape begins to shift as you descend from the mountains and approach the fjords. The final leg of the journey offers incredible views of rivers, valleys, and picturesque villages before reaching Bergen, where the mountains meet the sea.

Why Take the Train to Bergen?
A Scenic Adventure

The primary appeal of taking the train to Bergen is the unrivaled scenery along the route. This journey is often ranked among the most beautiful train rides in the world. The train travels through pristine wilderness areas, offering a chance to experience Norway's varied landscapes up close and without the distractions of city life. If you enjoy photography, this route will provide you with an abundance of opportunities to capture the natural beauty of the country.

Comfort and Relaxation

The trains on the Bergen Railway are designed for comfort, with spacious seats, air conditioning, free Wi-Fi, and power outlets at your disposal. This makes the journey not only a scenic experience but a relaxing one as well. You can sit back, read a book, or simply gaze out of the window as the countryside unfolds before you.

Connection to Other Norwegian Destinations

The Bergen Railway is a key part of Norway's rail network, so it offers a great connection to other cities and regions in the country. For example, you can easily combine your journey to Bergen with a trip to Oslo, Voss, or even other scenic fjord locations like **Aurland** or **Gudvangen**. The rail network in Norway is extensive, and train travel is one of the most efficient ways to see the country.

Train Services and Amenities

Vy operates the Bergen Railway, and their trains are equipped with modern amenities to ensure a comfortable ride. Some key features include:

- **Seating**: Trains feature comfortable, well-maintained seats, with both first-class and second-class options available. First-class passengers can enjoy additional services such as more spacious seating, newspapers, and complimentary snacks.
- **Wi-Fi**: Free Wi-Fi is available on board, allowing you to stay connected during the journey, check emails, or simply browse the internet while you enjoy the views.
- **Dining Options**: The train offers a small dining car where passengers can purchase snacks, coffee, and light meals. This is a great option if you get hungry during the journey.
- **Power Outlets**: Power outlets are available at each seat, allowing you to charge your devices as you travel.
- **Scenic Windows**: The trains are equipped with large windows that allow you to enjoy panoramic views of the Norwegian landscape. Be sure to sit on the right side of the train for the best views of the fjords and mountains.

Timetable and Frequency
Trains from Oslo to Bergen run several times a day, giving you flexibility in choosing a departure time. While there are no direct night trains on the Bergen Railway, there are early morning and late afternoon options that allow you to maximize your time in Bergen or Oslo.

- **Frequency**: Generally, there are 3-4 departures per day from **Oslo Central Station** to **Bergen Station**. The journey takes approximately 6.5 to 7 hours, with a few short breaks at stations such as Geilo and Finse.
- **Departure Times**: Trains typically depart in the morning (around 8:00 AM) and early afternoon (around 2:00 PM), but it's always best to check the Vy website for current schedules, as times may vary slightly depending on the season or specific day.

Prices and Tickets
Ticket prices for the Bergen Railway vary depending on the time of year, class of service, and how far in advance you book your ticket. It's always a good idea to book early, especially during peak tourist seasons, to secure the best rates.

- **Prices**: A one-way ticket from Oslo to Bergen in standard class typically ranges from **NOK 399 to NOK 799** (approximately **USD 40 to USD 80**) depending on how far in advance you book. First-class tickets are priced higher, with one-way fares typically ranging from **NOK 1,000 to NOK 1,500** (approximately **USD 100 to USD 150**).
- **Discounts**: Vy offers various discounts, including **youth tickets**, **senior discounts**, and **family packages**. You can also take advantage of **advance purchase deals** for lower prices if you book tickets early.
- **Ticket Booking**: Tickets can be easily booked on the Vy website, at ticket vending machines at Oslo Central Station, or through the Vy mobile app.

Additional Travel Tips

- **Luggage**: You can bring luggage on board the train, and there is ample space in dedicated luggage areas. Be sure to keep your valuables close by and use the overhead compartments for smaller bags.
- **Seating**: While seats are usually reserved for second-class tickets, it's recommended to book in advance if you're traveling during peak seasons (summer months or holidays).
- **Travel Insurance**: As with any long journey, consider purchasing travel insurance to cover any potential delays, cancellations, or unforeseen circumstances.
- **Snacks and Drinks**: While there is a dining car on the train, you may want to bring along some personal snacks or beverages to enjoy during the journey.

Taking the train to Bergen is not only a practical way to reach the city, but it is also an experience in itself. The scenic beauty, the comfort of the modern trains, and the chance to immerse yourself in Norway's stunning natural landscapes make this journey a highlight of your trip. Whether you're traveling from Oslo or connecting to the Bergen Railway from another part of Norway, the train ride offers a unique and unforgettable way to experience the charm of this remarkable country. Don't miss out on the opportunity to enjoy one of the world's most beautiful train rides as you make your way to Bergen!

How to Get to Bergen by Bus

Bergen, Norway, is a city renowned for its stunning fjords, scenic landscapes, and rich cultural history. While many travelers opt for trains or flights to reach this charming city, buses offer an alternative mode of transport that is often more affordable and offers unique scenic experiences along the way. Whether you're traveling from Oslo, Stavanger, or other Norwegian cities, a bus ride to Bergen can provide you with an excellent opportunity to relax, enjoy the views, and take in the Norwegian countryside. This guide will give you all the essential information you need to travel to Bergen by bus, including routes, amenities, and tips to make your journey smooth and enjoyable.

Major Bus Routes to Bergen

There are several bus companies that operate long-distance routes to Bergen from different parts of Norway. The most prominent of these are **Nettbuss** (now part of **Vy**), **Nor-Way Bussekspress**, and **Konkurrenten**. These companies offer multiple daily departures and flexible schedules to accommodate travelers from across the country. Here's a breakdown of the main routes to Bergen:

Oslo to Bergen by Bus

The journey between **Oslo** and **Bergen** is one of the most popular routes for bus travel in Norway. The trip covers approximately 460 kilometers (286 miles) and takes around **7.5 to 8 hours**, depending on traffic and the number of stops along the way. The buses traveling between these two cities typically provide comfort, air conditioning, Wi-Fi, and reclining seats, ensuring you have a pleasant journey.

- **Departure Points in Oslo**: The buses to Bergen typically depart from the **Oslo Bus Terminal**, which is centrally located near the Oslo Central Train Station. This terminal is a hub for multiple long-distance bus services, making it easy for travelers to find their buses and access other amenities such as shops and restrooms.

- **Arrival in Bergen**: The buses from Oslo will usually arrive at **Bergen Bus Station**, located just a short distance from the city center and the famous Bryggen waterfront area. The bus station offers easy connections to local buses and taxis, making it convenient to get around once you arrive in Bergen.

Stavanger to Bergen by Bus

If you're coming from **Stavanger**, the bus ride to Bergen takes approximately **5 to 6 hours**. This route is operated by **Nor-Way Bussekspress**, and the trip offers passengers spectacular views of the Norwegian coastline, fjords, and mountains. The Stavanger-Bergen bus route is ideal for travelers who wish to explore the scenic western region of Norway in a relaxed manner.

- **Departure Points in Stavanger**: Buses typically depart from **Stavanger Bus Station**, which is located in the city center and easily accessible by foot from popular attractions.
- **Arrival in Bergen**: Upon arrival at **Bergen Bus Station**, you'll be just minutes away from top attractions such as the UNESCO World Heritage-listed Bryggen, the bustling Fish Market, and the iconic Fløibanen funicular railway.

Other Routes to Bergen

There are also buses that connect Bergen with other Norwegian cities such as **Drammen**, **Voss**, and **Ålesund**. Depending on your departure point, the journey times vary, but most routes offer comfortable buses and picturesque landscapes. The frequency of bus services may vary, especially during off-peak seasons, so it's a good idea to check schedules in advance.

Features of Bus Travel to Bergen

When traveling by bus to Bergen, you can expect several key features and amenities that will enhance your journey. Here are some of the highlights:

Comfortable Seating

Buses that travel to Bergen are generally designed for long-distance comfort. The seats are spacious and come with ample legroom. Most buses feature **reclining seats**, allowing you to relax during the journey. Some services also offer seats with **extra legroom** in the front or premium cabins, which can be more comfortable for those who prefer a bit of extra space.

Onboard Wi-Fi and Charging Points

One of the major advantages of bus travel in Norway is the **free Wi-Fi** available on many buses. This allows you to stay connected with family and friends, catch up on work, or simply entertain yourself with movies, music, or games. Additionally, many buses offer **power outlets** or USB charging points at each seat, so you can charge your devices during the trip.

Air Conditioning and Restrooms

Comfortable air conditioning is available on almost all buses traveling to Bergen. This ensures a pleasant atmosphere, especially during the warmer summer months. Many buses are also equipped with **onboard restrooms**, making long journeys more convenient. Depending on the bus company, some services may also offer **refreshments** for purchase, such as water, coffee, and light snacks.

Scenic Views

Unlike other modes of transportation, the bus offers an excellent opportunity to see the landscape up close. Whether you are traveling from Oslo, Stavanger, or another city, the bus ride to Bergen will provide you with stunning views of Norwegian forests, fjords, lakes, and mountains. The journey also takes you through charming villages and towns, adding to the scenic experience.

How to Book Your Bus Ticket to Bergen

Booking a bus ticket to Bergen is relatively simple, with multiple options for purchasing tickets. Here's how to go about it:

Online Booking

Most bus companies, including **Vy**, **Nor-Way Bussekspress**, and **Konkurrenten**, offer **online booking** on their websites. You can easily browse schedules, select your departure time, and book tickets in advance. It's often cheaper to book online, as some companies offer discounts for early purchases.

- **Vy**: Vy operates several bus routes to Bergen, and tickets can be purchased through their official website or mobile app. Vy also provides real-time updates on bus schedules and seat availability.
- **Nor-Way Bussekspress**: For routes from cities like Stavanger and Oslo, you can visit the **Nor-Way Bussekspress** website to book tickets. This service offers multiple payment options, including credit card and PayPal.
- **Konkurrenten**: Konkurrenten also provides online booking for routes between cities like Bergen and Voss. Check their website for ticket information and available discounts.

Booking at the Bus Station

You can also buy tickets in person at the **Oslo Bus Terminal**, **Stavanger Bus Station**, or any other bus station in Norway that offers long-distance services. Most stations have ticket counters where you can purchase your ticket directly from the staff, or you can use automated machines to buy tickets for your trip.

Ticket Prices

Ticket prices vary depending on the route, time of travel, and how far in advance you book. On average, one-way tickets for the **Oslo to Bergen** route typically cost between **NOK 350 and NOK 600** (approximately **USD 35 to USD 60**), while tickets from **Stavanger to Bergen** range from **NOK 250 to NOK 450** (approximately **USD 25 to USD 45**). Keep in mind that ticket prices are usually lower if you book in advance or travel during off-peak hours.

Discounts and Special Offers

Many bus companies offer **discounts** for students, seniors, and children. Additionally, you may find **special promotions** or **package deals** that combine bus travel with local sightseeing tours or accommodation. Be sure to check each company's website for any available discounts or offers.

Travel Tips for Bus Journeys to Bergen

- **Arrive Early**: It's always a good idea to arrive at the bus station at least 15-20 minutes before departure, especially if you need to purchase your ticket or find your bus.
- **Pack Snacks and Drinks**: While buses often have onboard refreshments, it's a good idea to bring along your own snacks and drinks for the journey, especially if you're traveling for several hours.
- **Check the Weather**: The weather in Norway can change quickly, so pack accordingly. Bring a jacket, even during the warmer months, as temperatures in the mountains can be cooler than in the cities.
- **Be Prepared for Stops**: Long-distance buses make multiple stops along the way for rest breaks, refueling, and drop-offs. These stops usually last for 10 to 20 minutes, and they give you the chance to stretch your legs and grab a snack.
- **Plan Your Connections**: If you're connecting to another mode of transport, such as a ferry, train, or local bus, make sure to check the schedules to ensure you have enough time to transfer between services.

Traveling to Bergen by bus is an excellent option for those seeking a more affordable and scenic way to get to this spectacular Norwegian city. With comfortable buses, beautiful views along the way, and convenient schedules, bus travel offers a stress-free journey to Bergen. Whether you're coming from Oslo, Stavanger, or another city, the bus ride provides a relaxing way to experience Norway's stunning landscapes before you arrive at the historic city of Bergen.

Visa and travel requirements

Visa and Travel Requirements for Bergen, Norway

Traveling to Bergen, Norway, is an exciting experience, whether you're visiting for leisure, business, or other reasons. However, before embarking on your journey, it's essential to understand the **visa and travel requirements** to ensure a smooth and hassle-free arrival. Norway is a member of the **Schengen Area**, which means that travelers from many countries can enter without a visa. However, there are specific requirements depending on your nationality, the purpose of your visit, and the duration of your stay. This section will provide you with an in-depth overview of the visa and travel requirements for Bergen, Norway, in 2025.

Schengen Visa Overview

Norway is part of the **Schengen Area**, a group of European countries that have abolished border controls between each other. This means that if you're traveling to Norway, you may also be able to visit other Schengen countries (like Sweden, Denmark, and Finland) with the same visa. The **Schengen visa** is the most common visa required for short stays (up to 90 days) within this area.

Schengen Visa for Short Stays (Type C)

The Schengen visa allows you to stay in Norway and other Schengen countries for up to **90 days within a 180-day period**. This visa is typically issued for tourism, business, or family visits.

- **Validity**: The Schengen visa is usually valid for **single-entry**, **double-entry**, or **multiple-entry**, depending on your travel plans.
- **Application Process**: To apply for a Schengen visa to Norway, you must apply to the **Norwegian Embassy or Consulate** in your country of residence. In some cases, you may be required to apply through a **visa center** (VFS Global or other authorized agencies).
- **Documents Required**: The application process generally involves providing the following documents:
- A valid passport (with at least two blank pages) valid for at least **three months beyond your intended stay in Norway**.
- A completed visa application form.
- Recent passport-sized photographs that meet the required specifications.
- Proof of travel arrangements, such as flight reservations.
- Travel insurance with a minimum coverage of **€30,000** for medical emergencies and repatriation.
- Proof of accommodation in Bergen (hotel reservations, rental agreements, or invitation letters from hosts).
- Proof of sufficient financial means to cover your stay in Norway (bank statements, pay slips, etc.).
- A visa fee payment (typically between **€60-€80** depending on the nationality and type of visa).
- **Processing Time**: It's advisable to apply for a Schengen visa **at least 15 days before** your planned departure date, but no more than **6 months in advance**. Processing can take up to **15 calendar days**.

National Visa Exemptions (No Visa Required)
Certain nationalities do not require a visa to enter Norway for short stays (up to 90 days) within the Schengen Area. These countries are **visa-exempt** under the Schengen Agreement. If you're from one of these countries, you can travel to Bergen without needing a visa for tourism, business, or family visits.

Visa-Exempt Countries

The following countries' nationals do not need a visa for short stays (up to 90 days) in Norway:

- **European Union (EU)** and **European Economic Area (EEA)** countries: All citizens of EU/EEA countries can travel to Norway without a visa. This includes countries like Germany, France, Italy, Spain, and the Netherlands.
- **Nordic Countries**: Citizens of **Sweden, Finland, Denmark,** and **Iceland** can travel freely to Norway without a visa or residence permit.
- **Other Visa-Exempt Countries**: Countries like **United States, Canada, Australia, New Zealand, Japan, South Korea, Brazil,** and **Argentina** also enjoy visa-free access for short stays of up to 90 days within 180 days.

For travelers from **visa-exempt countries**, all you need is a valid passport or national ID card. However, your passport should be valid for at least **three months beyond the planned departure date**.

Exceptions for Longer Stays (More than 90 Days)

If you plan to stay in Norway for longer than **90 days**, even if you are from a visa-exempt country, you will need to apply for a **residence permit**. This is typically required for those traveling for **work, study, or family reunification** purposes.

Long-Term Stays and Residence Permits

If you plan to stay in Bergen for more than **90 days**, you will need to apply for a **residence permit** for Norway. This applies to individuals wishing to stay for work, studies, or family reunification.

Types of Residence Permits

There are several types of residence permits you may apply for, depending on the purpose of your stay:

- **Work Permit**: If you have secured a job in Norway, you will need to apply for a work permit. This permit requires you to have an offer from a Norwegian employer, and the specific requirements depend on the type of job and qualifications.
- **Study Permit**: If you are a student planning to study in Bergen, you will need a study permit. You must be accepted into a recognized educational institution and prove you have sufficient funds to support yourself during your stay.
- **Family Reunification**: If you are joining a family member in Norway, you may apply for a family reunification permit. This typically applies to spouses, children, or other close family members of Norwegian citizens or legal residents.

Application Process for Residence Permits

The process for applying for a residence permit varies depending on your situation. However, in most cases, you will need to submit an application to the **Norwegian Directorate of Immigration (UDI)**.

Documents Required: You will typically need to provide:

- A valid passport.
- Proof of your purpose for staying in Norway (job offer, university acceptance, family connection).
- Financial proof to demonstrate you can support yourself during your stay.
- Health insurance for the duration of your stay (if applicable).
- **Processing Time**: The processing time for residence permits can vary greatly, from a few weeks to several months, depending on the type of permit. It's important to apply as early as possible to avoid delays.

COVID-19 and Health-related Travel Restrictions

As of **2025**, the world continues to recover from the impact of the **COVID-19 pandemic**. Norway has put in place various **health-related travel restrictions** in response to global health concerns. These restrictions may change over time, so it is crucial to stay updated on the latest travel requirements before your trip.

- **Vaccination and Testing Requirements**: Depending on your country of departure and vaccination status, you may be required to present a **COVID-19 vaccination certificate** or a **negative test result** upon arrival in Norway.
- **Health Insurance**: All travelers to Norway are advised to have valid **travel health insurance** that covers COVID-19-related medical costs during their stay.

Be sure to check the **Norwegian government's official website** or the **Norwegian embassy** in your country for the latest health-related travel advice.

Customs Regulations and Currency

Customs Regulations

When traveling to Norway, it's important to understand the country's **customs regulations**. Norway is not part of the European Union, and thus it has its own customs rules:

- **Duty-Free Allowance**: Travelers from non-EU countries are allowed to bring in **duty-free goods**, including alcohol, tobacco, and perfume, within specified limits. For example, travelers over the age of 18 may bring in **1 liter of spirits** or **2 liters of wine** duty-free.
- **Prohibited Items**: Certain items, such as **drugs**, **weapons**, and **counterfeit goods**, are strictly prohibited from entering the country.

Currency and Payment Methods

The **Norwegian Krone (NOK)** is the official currency of Norway. While cash is still accepted, Norway is a highly digital country, and most transactions are made via **credit or debit cards**. It's advisable to carry a **small amount of cash** for emergencies or smaller establishments that may not accept cards.

- **ATMs**: Widely available in Bergen, and cards like **Visa** and **MasterCard** are accepted almost everywhere.
- **Currency Exchange**: Currency exchange services are available at **airports**, **banks**, and **exchange offices**.

Navigating the visa and travel requirements for Bergen, Norway, is essential to ensure a smooth and enjoyable trip. Depending on your nationality, the purpose of your visit, and the duration of your stay, you may require a Schengen visa, a residence permit, or simply your passport for entry. Always plan your travel well in advance, and make sure you are aware of any current travel restrictions or health requirements. With this knowledge, you're well on your way to experiencing the beauty and charm of Bergen.

Chapter 3. Top Attractions in Bergen

Bryggen Wharf

Bryggen Wharf, often referred to as the **old wharf** or the **historic dock area** in Bergen, is one of Norway's most iconic landmarks. Situated in the heart of the city along the picturesque harbor, Bryggen is a UNESCO World Heritage site and a testament to Bergen's rich history as a trading port. If you're planning to visit Bergen, exploring Bryggen Wharf is an absolute must. This area offers a fascinating glimpse into the past, with vibrant wooden buildings that evoke the charm of a bygone era.

Let's dive into a comprehensive and exhaustive guide to **Bryggen Wharf**—what to expect, what to explore, how to get there, and costs involved.

What to Expect at Bryggen Wharf

Historical Significance

Bryggen Wharf is not just a scenic spot; it holds immense historical significance. Once the center of the **Hanseatic League's trading empire**, the wharf was the hub of **medieval trade** between Norway and northern Europe. Established around the 12th century, the area became the focal point of commerce, particularly for the **Hanseatic merchants**—a powerful group of German traders who controlled a large portion of the trade in northern Europe from the 13th to the 17th century.

The buildings that stand today at Bryggen are largely reconstructed after a series of fires, the most devastating of which occurred in **1702**. Despite this, Bryggen has maintained its medieval charm, and its colorful wooden houses are still a testament to the past.

The buildings in Bryggen's wharf, with their gabled facades and narrow alleyways, are distinctive examples of traditional wooden Norwegian architecture. Their preservation is a nod to Bergen's long-standing maritime culture, and walking through the area offers a step back in time.

Atmosphere

Expect a lively yet serene atmosphere at Bryggen Wharf. During the day, it's filled with visitors exploring its historic buildings, museums, galleries, and shops. The area has an **authentic, vibrant feel** with its wooden facades, bustling galleries, and cozy cafés nestled between shops selling unique Norwegian crafts.

At night, Bryggen takes on a quieter, more peaceful ambiance, making it an excellent place for an evening stroll along the harbor. Whether you're visiting for a few hours or spending an entire day, Bryggen has a timeless appeal that captivates travelers of all kinds.

What to Explore at Bryggen Wharf

There's no shortage of fascinating things to do and see at Bryggen Wharf. Here's a breakdown of the main attractions:

Bryggen Museum

Located within the wharf, the **Bryggen Museum** offers visitors a chance to explore the history of the area and its significance to Bergen and Norway. It features fascinating exhibits that cover the **Hanseatic era**, medieval trade, and life in Bergen during the Middle Ages. You'll find artifacts like tools, furniture, and everyday items that showcase how the merchants lived and worked during that period.

- **What to Expect**: Interactive displays, archaeological findings, and historical exhibits about the Hanseatic League and medieval Bergen.
- **Cost**: Approximately **NOK 100** for adults, and discounted or free entry for children, seniors, and students.

Hanseatic Museum

The **Hanseatic Museum** is another important institution at Bryggen Wharf. It is housed in one of the original wooden buildings and offers an even more detailed insight into the Hanseatic merchants' life. The museum is a historical representation of the merchants' life in the 18th and 19th centuries, showcasing **furnishings**, **tools**, and **original artifacts**.

- **What to Expect**: Authentic interiors, artifacts from the Hanseatic period, and a glimpse into the **merchant culture** of medieval Bergen.
- **Cost**: Entry is usually around **NOK 100**, with some discounts for students and children.

The Old Wooden Buildings

The most famous feature of Bryggen Wharf is the **well-preserved wooden buildings**. Walking through these narrow, winding alleyways and between the tall buildings will give you a feeling of walking in medieval times. These buildings were once used as **warehouses**, **offices**, and **living spaces** for merchants, and many have been meticulously restored.

- **What to Expect**: Brightly colored facades, narrow alleys, and charming courtyards. You'll also find some of the oldest and most **authentic Norwegian architecture** still standing in the area.

Artisan Shops, Galleries, and Cafés

As you explore Bryggen Wharf, you'll find many **artisan shops**, **galleries**, and **cafés** housed within the old buildings. These establishments sell **local Norwegian goods**, such as **handmade woolen items**, **wooden crafts**, and **Norwegian art**. You can also enjoy the cozy cafés serving **Norwegian pastries** and **coffee** while soaking up the vibrant atmosphere.

- **What to Expect**: A variety of local arts and crafts, a perfect place to buy souvenirs or gifts. Many of the galleries feature **local artists**, showcasing everything from photography to modern Norwegian art.

Bryggen's Secret Alleys and Hidden Spots

While the main streets of Bryggen Wharf are quite popular, there are many **hidden alleyways** and **courtyards** to explore. These off-the-beaten-path spots offer a quieter experience where you can enjoy the beauty of Bryggen in solitude.

- **What to Expect**: Peaceful nooks, charming architecture, and a chance to experience the true essence of **Norwegian culture**.

How to Get to Bryggen Wharf
Getting There by Foot

Bryggen Wharf is situated right at the **harbor**, in the heart of Bergen. If you're already in the city center, it's a short walk to the wharf from virtually anywhere. From the **Bergen Railway Station**, Bryggen Wharf is only about **10-15 minutes** on foot.

- **What to Expect**: A scenic walk through cobbled streets, with many interesting shops, cafes, and street performances along the way.

Getting There by Public Transport

While Bergen's city center is compact, if you're coming from a more distant location, public transport is a viable option. You can take a **bus** to the **Bryggen area**, but keep in mind that walking is often more convenient and scenic. The **light rail** network, which started operations recently, can take you close to

Scan the QR code

1. **Open Camera:** Launch your smartphone's camera app.
2. **Position QR Code:** Place the QR code within the camera's viewfinder.
3. **Hold Steady:** Keep the device steady for the camera to focus.
4. **Wait for Scan:** Wait for the code to be recognized.
5. **Tap Notification:** Follow the prompt to access the content.

, but again, walking from stops such as **Bergen storsenter** is easy.

- **What to Expect**: Reliable and efficient local transport, but limited public transportation directly into Bryggen.

Parking

If you're driving, you can find **parking garages** near Bryggen Wharf. The **Bryggen parking lot** is one of the closest options. However, be aware that parking can be limited and expensive in this central location.

Cost of Visiting Bryggen Wharf

While walking around Bryggen Wharf and admiring the architecture is free, accessing museums and certain experiences requires an entry fee. Here's a breakdown of the expected costs:

- **Bryggen Museum**: Entry is around **NOK 100** for adults.
- **Hanseatic Museum**: Entry is about **NOK 100** for adults.
- **Walking Tours**: Guided walking tours around Bryggen and Bergen generally cost between **NOK 200-400** depending on the tour provider.
- **Souvenirs**: Prices in local shops and galleries vary, but expect to pay around **NOK 100-500** for unique crafts and artworks.

Bryggen Wharf in Bergen is one of the most iconic and historic locations in Norway, offering visitors a chance to experience the city's **rich maritime past**. Whether you're interested in its **history**, enjoying the **art galleries**, or simply soaking in the atmosphere of the old wooden buildings, Bryggen is a must-see. With easy access from the city center and a mix of free and paid attractions, Bryggen is an essential stop on any trip to Bergen.

Mount Fløyen and the Fløibanen Funicular

Mount **Fløyen** is one of Bergen's most beloved natural attractions, offering breathtaking panoramic views of the city, the harbor, and the surrounding fjords. Sitting at an elevation of **399 meters (1,309 feet)**, it provides visitors with an incredible vantage point for exploring the beauty of Bergen and the surrounding region. Accessing the top of Mount Fløyen is made easy by the **Fløibanen Funicular**, which transports visitors up the mountain in a smooth, comfortable ride.

If you're in Bergen and want to experience some of the most stunning natural landscapes Norway has to offer, a trip to Mount Fløyen is essential. Below is a comprehensive and exhaustive guide to this iconic location—what to expect, what to explore, how to get there, and the costs involved.

What to Expect at Mount Fløyen

Spectacular Views

The main draw of Mount Fløyen is undoubtedly its spectacular **views of Bergen**. From the top, visitors are treated to an unrivaled panoramic perspective of the city, the harbor, and the **surrounding mountains**. On a clear day, you can see as far as the **Hordatlanta fjord**, with the city's historic buildings, colorful wharves, and lush greenery all spread out beneath you. The view is especially stunning at sunset when the city lights begin to twinkle, casting a magical glow over the landscape.

- **What to Expect**: 360-degree views of Bergen's picturesque landscape, with breathtaking vistas of fjords, mountains, and the city. You can also spot landmarks like **Bryggen Wharf, the Bergenhus Fortress**, and **the Old Town**.

The Fløibanen Funicular

The **Fløibanen Funicular** is one of the oldest and most well-known funicular systems in the world, having been in operation since **1918**. It offers an **efficient and scenic way** to reach the summit of Mount Fløyen. The funicular's route is a **10-minute journey** that takes you up the mountain through **lush forests** and **scenic landscapes**, with several points along the way where you can enjoy stunning views of the city below.

- **What to Expect**: A smooth ride with occasional stops along the way to admire the views of Bergen and its surrounding mountains. It's an unforgettable experience that lets you soak in the beauty of the area while ascending to the peak.

The Scenic Walks and Hiking Trails

Once you reach the top of Mount Fløyen, there are several hiking trails and scenic walking routes to explore. These trails cater to all levels of ability, from easy walks around the summit to more challenging hikes into the mountains and forests surrounding Fløyen. The **Fløyen to Ulriken trail**, which connects Mount Fløyen to another iconic peak in Bergen, **Mount Ulriken**, is popular among avid hikers.

- **What to Expect**: A variety of walking paths, including **easy strolls** along the summit with paved pathways, and more **challenging hiking routes** through the mountains for those looking for a longer adventure. Some trails are equipped with resting spots and signs explaining the area's flora and fauna.

What to Explore at Mount Fløyen

There's much more to do at Mount Fløyen than just enjoying the views. Here are some of the key attractions:

The Fløyen Viewpoint

At the summit of Mount Fløyen, you'll find several viewpoints where you can take in the stunning panoramas. The **Fløyen Viewpoint** is the perfect spot to sit, relax, and snap some photos of Bergen. Whether you visit in the winter to see the snowy landscape or during the summer months to enjoy the lush greenery, the views from here are always incredible.

- **What to Expect**: A panoramic outlook that allows you to view Bergen in all its glory, from the **mountains** and **harbor** to the **city center** and the **surrounding islands**.

The Fløibanen Station and Visitor Center

At the top, there's a **Fløibanen Station** and visitor center where you can learn more about the funicular system, its history, and the surrounding area. The center features an exhibition on the **history of the funicular** and offers information on **hiking trails**, **tourist activities**, and **weather conditions** in the region.

- **What to Expect**: An informative and helpful visitor center, where you can gain insight into Bergen's natural and cultural attractions. It's also a great place to pick up **maps** and **brochures** for hiking and outdoor adventures.

Mount Fløyen Café

After a day of exploring, head to the **Mount Fløyen Café**, where you can enjoy hot drinks, freshly baked pastries, and light meals. The café is a cozy spot to relax and enjoy a bite while taking in the magnificent views of Bergen. It's an ideal place to unwind after a hike or funicular ride.

- **What to Expect**: A cozy café offering local Norwegian pastries, warm beverages, and delicious food with sweeping views of the surrounding landscape.

Playgrounds and Family-Friendly Activities

Mount Fløyen is also a family-friendly destination, with activities for children. One of the highlights is the **playground** at the summit, which features swings, slides, and climbing structures for kids to enjoy while parents can relax with a view. During the winter months, the area is also a popular spot for **sledging** and **snow activities**.

- **What to Expect**: A well-maintained playground with ample space for kids to play, alongside a safe and family-oriented environment with a variety of activities for all ages.

Fløyen's Wildlife and Nature

Mount Fløyen is not just about the views—it's also home to a rich ecosystem of **wildlife** and **nature**. The surrounding forests and mountains are home to a variety of birds, plants, and animals. If you enjoy nature walks or birdwatching, there are plenty of opportunities to spot local wildlife such as **roe deer**, **squirrels**, and an array of **Norwegian bird species**.

- **What to Expect**: A chance to experience Norway's natural beauty with local flora and fauna, making it an ideal spot for nature enthusiasts.

How to Get to Mount Fløyen
Getting There by Funicular (Fløibanen)

The easiest and most popular way to reach the summit of Mount Fløyen is by riding the **Fløibanen Funicular**. The funicular departs regularly from **Bergen's city center**, specifically from **Fløibanen Station** on **Vetrlidsalmen Street**. The ride takes about **5-10 minutes**, offering scenic views as you ascend.

- **What to Expect**: A short and comfortable journey with impressive views of Bergen as you ascend to the top. The funicular operates **year-round**, making it accessible in all seasons.

Getting There by Foot

If you're feeling adventurous and enjoy hiking, you can also reach Mount Fløyen by foot. There are a few **walking paths** from the city center to the summit, though these hikes can take anywhere from **30 minutes to an hour** depending on your pace.

- **What to Expect**: A more strenuous but rewarding walk, offering the chance to explore Bergen's urban and natural landscapes as you make your way to the top.

Cost of Visiting Mount Fløyen and the Fløibanen Funicular

While visiting Mount Fløyen and enjoying its natural beauty is free, the **Fløibanen Funicular** requires a ticket. Here are the costs:

Fløibanen Funicular Ticket Prices

- **Adult Return Ticket**: Approximately **NOK 100-130**
- **Child Return Ticket (6-16 years)**: Approximately **NOK 40-70**
- **Family Ticket (2 adults + 2 children)**: Approximately **NOK 250-300**
- **Single Ticket (one way)**: Approximately **NOK 50-70**

The **Fløibanen Funicular** offers a discount for children and families, making it affordable for visitors of all ages. Tickets can be purchased at the station or online for convenience.

Additional Costs

If you plan on using the **hiking trails** or visiting the **Mount Fløyen Café**, expect prices for food and drink to be around **NOK 50-150** per item, depending on what you order.

Mount Fløyen and the Fløibanen Funicular are two of Bergen's most popular and breathtaking attractions. Whether you're visiting for the incredible views, the outdoor activities, or the chance to experience nature up close, Fløyen offers something for everyone. Its accessibility by funicular makes it easy to reach, and the variety of trails and family-friendly amenities ensures that your visit will be unforgettable. Whether you're taking a funicular ride, hiking through the forests, or simply relaxing at the summit, Mount Fløyen is a must-see when visiting Bergen.

Bergenhus Fortress

Bergenhus Fortress, one of the oldest and best-preserved fortifications in Norway, is a must-visit destination for history enthusiasts and anyone interested in exploring Bergen's rich cultural heritage. Situated at the entrance to the Bergen harbor, the fortress offers visitors an opportunity to step back in time and discover the military and royal history that helped shape the city.

This guide provides an exhaustive overview of Bergenhus Fortress, including what to expect, what to explore, how to get there, and the costs involved.

What to Expect at Bergenhus Fortress

Bergenhus Fortress is a remarkable blend of military history, architectural grandeur, and scenic surroundings. The fortress complex consists of several historic buildings, including royal residences, military structures, and defensive walls. It sits on a strategic location, overlooking the harbor, and has served various purposes throughout its long history.

Historical Significance

Bergenhus Fortress has a rich and storied past that dates back to the **13th century**, originally constructed by **King Haakon IV** of Norway. It was initially designed as a royal residence and a military stronghold to protect the city and its strategic harbor. Over the centuries, the fortress underwent numerous expansions and modifications, and it became a central point for the defense of Bergen.

- **What to Expect**: The fortress offers visitors the chance to explore centuries of history, from its medieval roots to its use as a military installation during various wars. You'll be walking through the same courtyards and halls where Norwegian kings and military leaders once stood.

Stunning Views of Bergen

Bergenhus Fortress provides some of the most stunning views of **Bergen's harbor** and surrounding areas. Whether you're enjoying the view from the top of the fortress walls or strolling through its gardens, the picturesque backdrop of the city's waterfront, the fjords, and the mountains will captivate you.

- **What to Expect**: A perfect spot for photo opportunities, especially if you're keen on capturing the natural beauty of Bergen in contrast to the fortress's architectural grandeur.

What to Explore at Bergenhus Fortress

Bergenhus Fortress is more than just a military installation—it's a treasure trove of historical landmarks, architectural wonders, and cultural gems. Here are some of the highlights you can explore within the fortress complex:

Haakon's Hall (Håkonshallen)

One of the most iconic structures within Bergenhus Fortress is **Haakon's Hall**. Built in the early **13th century**, this majestic building was once the royal residence of Norwegian kings and served as the location for grand events like feasts, ceremonies, and meetings. Haakon's Hall is renowned for its impressive architecture, particularly its **stunning medieval hall** and **large vaulted ceilings**.

- **What to Expect**: An awe-inspiring room where Norwegian kings held court. The hall is still used for special occasions and is often open to visitors who want to admire its historical architecture. There are **guided tours** available that offer detailed information about the hall's history and its significance in Norway's royal heritage.

The Rosenkrantz Tower (Rosenkrantztårnet)

The **Rosenkrantz Tower** is another key feature of Bergenhus Fortress. Named after the 16th-century nobleman **Steen Rosenkrantz**, who oversaw its expansion, this tower was used for both defensive and residential purposes. The tower houses the remains of a **medieval castle**, a **fortified residence**, and a **military garrison**.

- **What to Expect**: The tower offers a fascinating glimpse into the architectural evolution of the fortress. The interior includes **historic rooms, medieval artifacts**, and even a **dungeon**. Visitors can also ascend to the top of the tower, where they can enjoy panoramic views of the city, harbor, and surrounding mountains.

The Fortress Walls and Defense Structures

The fortress is also home to some of the most well-preserved defensive structures in Norway, including its massive walls, gates, and bastions. These fortifications were designed to protect Bergen from invading forces and served as a strategic military point for centuries.

- **What to Expect**: You can explore the various fortifications that make up the perimeter of the fortress, including its **defensive walls**, **watch towers**, and **canons**. Some of the walls date back to the **14th century**, providing a rare opportunity to see medieval military architecture firsthand.

The Fortress Courtyard

The **fortress courtyard** is an open space where visitors can walk freely, admire the architecture, and enjoy the peaceful atmosphere of the site. It is also the location for various **historical reenactments** and events throughout the year.

- **What to Expect**: A tranquil space filled with greenery and a mix of old stone structures. The courtyard is often the site of public gatherings, medieval festivals, and exhibitions related to Bergen's history.

How to Get to Bergenhus Fortress
Bergenhus Fortress is located in the heart of Bergen, right at the entrance to the harbor, making it easy to reach from most parts of the city. Here are the main ways to get there:

Getting There by Foot

The fortress is a short walk from **Bergen's city center**, and many visitors choose to explore it on foot. If you're staying in central Bergen, the walk to the fortress will take about **10-15 minutes**.

- **What to Expect**: A pleasant walk along the harbor, passing scenic views of Bergen's old town and waterfront. It's a perfect way to experience the city's charm as you head toward the fortress.

Getting There by Bus

Several **local buses** and **public transport routes** serve the area around Bergenhus Fortress. The **bus station near the fortress** is **Bergen Storsenter**, which is just a short walk from the entrance. You can easily reach this station by taking **bus routes 2, 3, or 4** from the city center.

- **What to Expect**: A quick and easy ride, especially if you are traveling from one of the farther districts of Bergen. Buses are regular and reliable.

Getting There by Car

If you're driving, Bergenhus Fortress is easily accessible from Bergen's city center. There are several parking lots and **street parking** options near the fortress.

Scan the QR code

1. **Open Camera:** Launch your smartphone's camera app.
2. **Position QR Code:** Place the QR code within the camera's viewfinder.
3. **Hold Steady:** Keep the device steady for the camera to focus.
4. **Wait for Scan:** Wait for the code to be recognized.
5. **Tap Notification:** Follow the prompt to access the content.

- **What to Expect**: A few minutes' drive from Bergen's central shopping areas. Note that parking spaces can be limited, especially during peak tourist seasons.

Cost of Visiting Bergenhus Fortress

Visiting Bergenhus Fortress is a relatively affordable experience, with entry fees primarily applying to the key buildings like Haakon's Hall and Rosenkrantz Tower. Below are the costs you can expect:

Ticket Prices

- **Adults**: Approximately **NOK 100-120** for access to Haakon's Hall and Rosenkrantz Tower.
- **Children (under 16)**: Free entry to the fortress and its grounds, though they will need a ticket for the buildings.
- **Seniors (over 67)**: Approximately **NOK 80-100**.
- **Families**: Family tickets are often available for a reduced rate, typically around **NOK 250-350** for two adults and two children.

Guided Tours

For those who want a deeper understanding of the history of the fortress, **guided tours** are available. These tours typically cost around **NOK 150-200** per person and last around **45-60 minutes**. The guides offer insightful commentary on the history of Bergenhus Fortress, the various buildings, and the role the fortress played in the city's defense.

Bergenhus Fortress is a key historical and cultural landmark in Bergen, offering visitors the chance to explore centuries of military history, royal architecture, and scenic beauty. Whether you're admiring the views from the Rosenkrantz Tower, exploring Haakon's Hall, or strolling through the fortress walls, a visit to Bergenhus is an opportunity to immerse yourself in the past while enjoying one of the most iconic sites in Norway. The fortress is accessible and affordable, making it a must-see attraction for anyone visiting Bergen in 2025.

Fantoft Stave Church

Fantoft Stave Church, a remarkable piece of Norway's architectural heritage, is a must-visit destination for anyone interested in the country's medieval history and unique wooden construction. Situated on the outskirts of Bergen, this reconstructed church provides visitors with a chance to explore a vital piece of Norwegian cultural history. This guide offers an exhaustive look at Fantoft Stave Church, including what to expect, what to explore, how to get there, and the costs involved.

What to Expect at Fantoft Stave Church

Fantoft Stave Church is a striking example of traditional **Norwegian stave church architecture**, known for its wooden construction and intricate carvings. The church was originally built in the **12th century**, and while the original structure no longer stands, it was meticulously reconstructed in the **1990s** after it was tragically burned down by arsonists in **1992**.

Architectural Features

The church is built in the classic **stave church style**, which uses large wooden staves (posts) to support the structure. The exterior is adorned with **ornate carvings**, dragon motifs, and pointed roofs, typical of medieval Viking-inspired architecture. The building is a visual masterpiece, combining both elegance and strength in its design.

- **What to Expect**: A blend of old-world craftsmanship and artistry. You'll see the typical **decorative dragons** and **Viking motifs** that characterize many Norwegian stave churches, as well as the **stunning woodwork** that defines the style. The church's exterior features steep roofs and sharp gables, making it a standout architectural treasure.

The Interior

Inside the church, the space is designed with simplicity and elegance, befitting its medieval origins. The church's interior is modest but beautifully crafted, with wooden benches, a pulpit, and detailed carvings around the altar area.

- **What to Expect**: The interior is calm and serene, with **high wooden beams** that create a lofty feel. There are several **religious motifs**, including **biblical scenes** carved into the woodwork, and the intricate **wooden ceiling** adds to the spiritual atmosphere. You'll find that the interior design evokes the spiritual significance of the church while showcasing the craftsmanship of the time.

The Surroundings

Fantoft Stave Church is located in a scenic area surrounded by lush forests, providing a peaceful and reflective atmosphere for visitors. The church grounds feature walking paths and are located near **Lake Storetveit**, making it an ideal spot for photography and leisurely walks.

- **What to Expect**: A tranquil setting that allows you to immerse yourself in the beauty of nature and the historical significance of the church. The surrounding area is perfect for peaceful walks or enjoying a quiet moment in the shadow of the church.

What to Explore at Fantoft Stave Church

Fantoft Stave Church is more than just a religious site—it's a museum and a cultural landmark that offers plenty for visitors to explore.

The Church's History and Reconstruction

One of the most fascinating aspects of Fantoft Stave Church is its history of destruction and reconstruction. The original church was built in **1150** and stood for centuries before being destroyed by fire in **1992**. The church was later reconstructed using traditional methods, closely following the original design and structure. This process took several years and involved meticulous research into the church's history and architecture.

- **What to Expect**: Inside the church, you'll find information about its origins, its destruction, and its reconstruction, including photos of the original church and detailed explanations of how it was rebuilt. The reconstruction project is a testament to the dedication to preserving Norway's cultural heritage.

The Carvings and Iconography

The stave church is adorned with **intricate wooden carvings**, some of which depict **religious stories** from the Bible, while others are based on Viking mythology. These carvings are typical of the stave church tradition, where artisans would often combine Christian and pagan motifs into a unique artistic expression.

- **What to Expect**: As you walk around the church, take time to examine the fine carvings. You'll notice **dragons**, **crosses**, and **scenes from the Bible**. The church's wooden design is almost like an open-air gallery, showcasing the interplay between faith, culture, and artistry.

The Church's Role in Norwegian History

Fantoft Stave Church was originally located in the village of **Fantoft**, and it played an essential role in the religious and cultural life of the area. The church was eventually moved to its current location in **1997**, where it now stands as a vital part of Norwegian history. The church's journey, from a humble village church to a world-famous icon of Norwegian heritage, is an important part of its story.

- **What to Expect**: Learn about the church's historical context and its role in the evolution of Christian architecture in Norway. You'll discover how stave churches were used for centuries as places of worship, community gathering, and local culture.

How to Get to Fantoft Stave Church

Fantoft Stave Church is located in the **Fantoft area** of Bergen, about **6 km south of the city center**, and it's easily accessible by public transport, car, and bike.

Getting There by Public Transport

- **By Bus**: You can take **bus 3** or **bus 35** from Bergen city center to reach Fantoft Stave Church. The journey takes around **15-20 minutes**, and the stop is just a short walk from the church.
- **By Light Rail**: If you prefer the light rail, take the **Bybanen Line** 1 from the city center toward **Nesttun**. The closest station to the church is **Fantoft Station**, which is located within walking distance of the church.
- **What to Expect**: A quick and affordable journey to the church, with regular bus and light rail services that make it easy to get to the site. Be sure to check schedules in advance to avoid long waiting times.

Getting There by Car

If you're driving, Fantoft Stave Church is located off the main roads and is easily accessible by car from the Bergen city center. There is **free parking** available near the church for visitors.

- **What to Expect**: A short, scenic drive through Bergen's outskirts, with plenty of parking available at the church grounds.

Getting There by Bike

For those who enjoy cycling, the route to Fantoft Stave Church is bike-friendly, and you can cycle from the city center in about **30 minutes**.

- **What to Expect**: A pleasant bike ride through the suburbs of Bergen, with easy-to-follow paths and scenic views of the countryside and surrounding areas.

Cost of Visiting Fantoft Stave Church

Visiting Fantoft Stave Church is a relatively affordable experience, and the costs depend on the type of visit you prefer. Here's a breakdown of the ticket prices:

General Admission

- **Adults**: Around **NOK 60-80** for a general admission ticket.
- **Children (under 16)**: Free entry.
- **Seniors (over 67)**: Approximately **NOK 40-60**.

Guided Tours

Guided tours are available for visitors who want a more in-depth experience. The tours typically cost around **NOK 150-200** per person, lasting approximately **45-60 minutes**.

- **What to Expect**: The guided tour will take you through the history and architectural significance of the church, including details about its reconstructions and the cultural importance of stave churches in Norwegian history.

Fantoft Stave Church is a unique and stunning historical landmark that showcases the finest elements of Norwegian craftsmanship and cultural heritage. Whether you are a history buff, an architecture enthusiast, or simply looking to experience one of Norway's most beautiful and serene locations, a visit to Fantoft Stave Church will leave you awe-struck. With its remarkable wooden carvings, rich history, and tranquil setting, Fantoft Stave Church is a must-visit destination in Bergen for 2025.

Chapter 4. Exploring the Scenic Fjords

The Sognefjord: Norway's longest and deepest

The **Sognefjord**, known as Norway's longest and deepest fjord, is one of the country's most awe-inspiring natural wonders. Stretching over **200 kilometers** inland and reaching depths of over **1,300 meters**, it is often referred to as the **"King of the Fjords"** due to its vastness and grandeur. With its towering cliffs, crystal-clear waters, and charming villages nestled along its shores, the Sognefjord is a place where the power of nature can be felt in every view and every experience. In this comprehensive guide, we explore everything there is to know about visiting the Sognefjord, from what to expect, how to get there, to the activities and experiences that will make your trip unforgettable.

What to Expect at the Sognefjord

When you visit the Sognefjord, you will encounter one of the most spectacular landscapes in the world. The fjord is a mixture of dramatic cliffs, waterfalls, lush green valleys, and pristine waters, offering an almost surreal beauty. As you travel through this majestic natural formation, you'll encounter diverse views and settings, each more mesmerizing than the last.

Magnificent Landscape and Scenic Views

The Sognefjord's striking landscape includes everything from steep mountainsides with waterfalls cascading down into the fjord below, to remote islands and small coastal villages dotted along its shores. The fjord is surrounded by snow-capped peaks, and the lush green valleys provide an astonishing contrast to the rugged, rocky cliffs that rise dramatically out of the water.

- **What to Expect**: As you journey along the fjord, you will be surrounded by towering mountains, deep waters, and the peaceful calm that defines the region. The ever-changing landscape will provide numerous opportunities for breathtaking photos, especially if you travel by boat or take a scenic drive along the fjord's edge.

Crystal-Clear Waters

One of the most remarkable features of the Sognefjord is its stunning, crystal-clear waters. The fjord's water is so pure that, in some areas, you can see straight to the bottom, even at significant depths. The water's pristine condition is the result of the natural filtration processes of the surrounding mountains, and the fjord itself is a haven for marine life.

- **What to Expect**: When you gaze at the water, you will notice its glass-like appearance, creating a perfect mirror reflection of the surrounding landscape. On a clear day, the blue water contrasts beautifully with the green of the forests and the white of the snow-covered mountains.

Small Villages and Communities

The Sognefjord is not only about dramatic nature but also about the charming human settlements that have lived in harmony with the landscape for centuries. Small, picturesque villages like **Flåm**, **Gudvangen**, and **Balestrand** are scattered throughout the fjord, offering a glimpse into Norwegian life in these remote and serene areas. Many of these villages are accessible by boat, making them ideal stopovers for travelers who want to explore local culture, architecture, and hospitality.

- **What to Expect**: As you cruise or drive along the fjord, you will pass quaint villages, each offering unique attractions. These communities are known for their **traditional wooden houses**, **local crafts**, and **welcoming residents**, making them the perfect spots to take a break and immerse yourself in the local lifestyle.

Activities and Experiences at the Sognefjord

The Sognefjord is not just about admiring its beauty from afar; there are plenty of exciting and immersive activities for visitors to enjoy. Whether you're an adventure seeker, nature enthusiast, or history buff, the fjord offers something for everyone.

Boat Tours

One of the most popular ways to explore the Sognefjord is by boat. You can take a **traditional fjord cruise**, a **high-speed RIB boat ride**, or even rent a private boat to explore the fjord at your own pace. Boat tours allow you to see the fjord from the water, providing you with some of the best views of the towering cliffs and lush shores.

- **What to Expect**: On a boat tour, you'll glide along the calm waters of the fjord, passing dramatic landscapes, waterfalls, and small islands. Some tours even offer stops at key attractions, such as **Kjenndal Glacier, Nærøyfjord**, and the **Flåm Railway**. Depending on the tour, you may also be able to kayak or paddleboard in the fjord for a more personal experience.

Hiking and Trekking

If you're a hiking enthusiast, the Sognefjord region offers some of Norway's most beautiful and challenging trails. The surrounding mountains offer fantastic trekking opportunities, with trails that range from easy walks to more challenging hikes that take you to the top of the fjord's cliffs for panoramic views.

- **What to Expect**: You can take moderate hikes to spots like the **Stalheimskleiva**, which is the steepest mountain road in Norway, or opt for the **Romsdalseggen Ridge** hike, which offers breathtaking views of the fjord and surrounding valleys. Along the way, you will be immersed in the untouched wilderness, surrounded by alpine meadows, forests, and rushing rivers.

The Flåm Railway

For those who want to experience the fjord from a different perspective, the **Flåm Railway** is a world-famous scenic train ride that takes you through some of the most dramatic landscapes in Norway. The train departs from the village of Flåm and takes passengers on a 20-kilometer journey up the mountainside, passing waterfalls, forests, and steep valleys along the way.

- **What to Expect**: On this unforgettable journey, you will be able to witness the fjord from above, with the train winding its way through narrow tunnels and across high bridges. The **Kjosfossen waterfall** is one of the highlights of the trip, where the train stops to allow passengers to marvel at the cascading water.

Kayaking and Canoeing

For a more active and intimate way to explore the fjord, consider **kayaking** or **canoeing**. This activity lets you paddle through the calm waters of the fjord, getting up close to the towering cliffs and secluded beaches that line the shores.

- **What to Expect**: You'll have the chance to explore hidden coves, secret beaches, and serene inlets, making this a perfect activity for nature lovers and those looking for a peaceful experience. Guided tours are available for first-time kayakers, but you can also rent equipment and explore on your own.

Cultural and Historical Experiences

While the Sognefjord is best known for its natural beauty, the region also offers a rich cultural and historical backdrop. The surrounding villages are steeped in history, and you can visit several local museums and sites that tell the story of the area's past.

- **What to Expect**: You can visit the **Viking Museum** in Gudvangen, explore the **Sogn Folk Museum** in Kaupanger, or learn about Norway's **Stave Churches**, such as the **Hopperstad Stave Church** in Vik. These experiences will give you insight into the area's Viking heritage, the local way of life, and the region's evolution over the centuries.

The Sognefjord

Scan the QR code

1. **Open Camera:** Launch your smartphone's camera app.
2. **Position QR Code:** Place the QR code within the camera's viewfinder.
3. **Hold Steady:** Keep the device steady for the camera to focus.
4. **Wait for Scan:** Wait for the code to be recognized.
5. **Tap Notification:** Follow the prompt to access the content.

How to Get to the Sognefjord

The Sognefjord is located in the heart of Norway and can be easily accessed from Bergen, Oslo, or other nearby cities.

By Car

Driving is one of the best ways to explore the Sognefjord, as it allows you to take in the stunning views at your own pace. The **E16 highway** connects Bergen to the Sognefjord, making it easy to drive from the city to the fjord in about **4-5 hours**. If you prefer a scenic route, consider taking the **Rv55** road, which provides more spectacular views of the fjord and the surrounding mountains.

By Train

Norway has an excellent rail network, and you can take a **train** from Oslo or Bergen to **Myrdal**, where you can switch to the **Flåm Railway** for a scenic ride down into the heart of the fjord. Trains from Bergen to Myrdal take about **2.5 hours**, while the journey from Oslo to Myrdal takes **4-5 hours**.

By Boat

From Bergen, you can take a **cruise** or **ferry** into the Sognefjord. These options provide an immersive experience of the fjord's beauty, as you can enjoy breathtaking views along the way.

Costs of Visiting the Sognefjord

The cost of visiting the Sognefjord depends on the activities and experiences you choose. Here is a general breakdown of prices:

- **Boat tours**: Prices range from **NOK 250 to NOK 1,500** depending on the tour type and duration.
- **Flåm Railway tickets**: Adult tickets typically range from **NOK 500 to NOK 800** for a one-way journey.
- **Kayak rentals**: Around **NOK 250-500** per day for a single kayak.
- **Hiking**: Free, though guided hikes may cost **NOK 200-400**.
- **Train tickets**: From Bergen to Flåm, tickets generally cost **NOK 400-600** one-way.

Visiting the **Sognefjord** in 2025 promises to be an experience that will leave you in awe of nature's power and

beauty. With its diverse landscapes, charming villages, and abundance of activities, the Sognefjord offers a truly unforgettable journey through Norway's majestic wilderness. Whether you're hiking along its cliffs, sailing on its waters, or simply enjoying the tranquility of the surrounding fjord, this incredible destination is a must-visit for anyone looking to experience the best of Norway.

Hardangerfjord: The Orchard of Norway

Nestled in the heart of Norway, **Hardangerfjord** is often referred to as the "Orchard of Norway" due to its lush fruit orchards that line the fjord's shores. This picturesque region, with its stunning combination of natural beauty, vibrant orchards, and charming villages, is one of Norway's most beloved destinations. Spanning over **179 kilometers**, Hardangerfjord is the second longest fjord in Norway and offers a wealth of activities and experiences, from hiking and boating to exploring cultural sites. This comprehensive guide will take you through everything you need to know about visiting Hardangerfjord, including what to expect, how to get there, and the incredible experiences that await you.

What to Expect at Hardangerfjord

Hardangerfjord is a breathtaking landscape that offers a combination of dramatic nature, cultural heritage, and a unique climate. The fjord is known for its mild climate, which allows orchards of apples, pears, and cherries to thrive in the region. As you approach the fjord, you will be greeted by stunning views of crystal-clear waters, towering mountains, and the colorful blossoms that define this unique part of Norway.

1.1 Scenic Landscape and Spectacular Views

The fjord is surrounded by steep mountainsides that rise dramatically from the water, while lush forests, waterfalls, and charming villages dot the landscape. One of the most iconic views is of **Hardangerjøkulen**, the glacier at the head of the fjord, which adds a surreal touch to the already stunning environment.

- **What to Expect**: As you explore Hardangerfjord, you'll encounter a variety of landscapes, from rugged cliffs and majestic waterfalls like **Vøringsfossen** to the peaceful, idyllic orchards that stretch out in the fertile valleys. The contrast between the glacial peaks and the blooming orchards creates a stunning visual harmony, particularly in spring and summer.

The Orchards: Nature's Bounty

Hardangerfjord is famous for its abundant fruit orchards. The fjord is often referred to as the "**Orchard of Norway**" due to its fertile soil, which supports the growth of apples, pears, and cherries. In spring, the orchards are covered with delicate blossoms, creating an explosion of colors that are simply mesmerizing.

- **What to Expect**: Depending on the time of your visit, you'll either see the orchards in full bloom (spring) or in harvest season (late summer to fall). The fruit harvests are celebrated with festivals, and visitors can purchase fresh local produce or taste fruit-based products such as apple cider and juice.

Activities and Experiences at Hardangerfjord

Hardangerfjord offers a wide range of activities for nature lovers, adventure seekers, and those who simply want to immerse themselves in the region's unique culture. Whether you're hiking in the mountains, exploring the villages, or enjoying the fjord on a boat tour, there's something for everyone to enjoy.

Boat Tours and Cruises

One of the best ways to explore Hardangerfjord is by boat. Several boat tours and cruises operate along the fjord, giving visitors the opportunity to experience the majestic beauty of the fjord from the water. You can enjoy everything from a **classic fjord cruise** to a **private boat tour** that takes you through the serene waters and past charming villages.

- **What to Expect**: On a boat tour, you'll cruise through the calm waters, passing waterfalls, islands, and fjordside villages. Many boat tours also stop at local villages, giving you the chance to explore the area on foot and sample regional delicacies.

Hiking and Trekking

Hardangerfjord is an excellent destination for hiking and trekking. The fjord region offers numerous trails, ranging from gentle walks through the orchards to more challenging hikes that lead to high-altitude vistas overlooking the fjord. The **Hardangervidda National Park** is a major attraction for hikers, offering a variety of trails suitable for all levels of experience.

- **What to Expect**: On a hike in Hardangerfjord, you will encounter diverse landscapes, including alpine meadows, dense forests, and dramatic cliffs. Popular hiking destinations include the **Vøringsfossen waterfall**, **Rembesdalen Valley**, and **Hardangervidda**, which is one of Europe's largest mountain plateaus. For a challenging hike, consider summiting **Mount Hårteigen**, which offers spectacular views of the surrounding fjords.

Fruit Picking and Orchard Tours

During the fruit harvest season, visitors can experience life in the orchards by participating in **fruit picking**. Some farms offer guided tours where visitors can learn about the history of the orchards and the production of fruit-based products such as apple juice, cider, and jam.

- **What to Expect**: Depending on the time of year, you can stroll through orchards in full bloom or participate in fruit-picking activities, where you can gather apples, pears, and cherries. Visitors are also encouraged to sample fresh fruit and visit local farms to learn more about the production process.

Cultural and Historical Experiences

Hardangerfjord is home to several cultural and historical sites, including **traditional wooden churches** and **local museums** that tell the story of the region's history, culture, and agricultural practices. The area also has a rich Viking history, with archaeological sites and heritage museums offering insight into life in the region hundreds of years ago.

- **What to Expect**: A visit to the **Hardanger Folk Museum** or **Norwegian Museum of Hydropower and Industry** will provide you with a deeper understanding of the region's history and industrial developments. You can also visit the **Kinsarvik Stave Church**, one of the oldest stave churches in the country, or explore the Viking sites in the surrounding area.

Festivals and Local Events

Hardangerfjord is known for its lively festivals, many of which revolve around the fruit harvest. The **Hardanger Fruit Festival** is held every year to celebrate the orchard harvest, with a variety of activities such as fruit tasting, traditional Norwegian music, and cultural performances.

- **What to Expect**: During festivals, you'll have the opportunity to try local foods, participate in games and activities, and enjoy traditional Norwegian entertainment. The festivals provide a great chance to interact with locals and experience the cultural vibrancy of the region.

Scan the QR code
1. Open Camera: Launch your smartphone's camera app.
2. Position QR Code: Place the QR code within the camera's viewfinder.
3. Hold Steady: Keep the device steady for the camera to focus.
4. Wait for Scan: Wait for the code to be recognized.
5. Tap Notification: Follow the prompt to access the content.

How to Get to Hardangerfjord

Hardangerfjord is located in **Vestland County**, in the southwestern part of Norway. The region is easily accessible from Bergen, making it a popular day trip or weekend getaway for visitors exploring western Norway.

By Car

Driving to Hardangerfjord from Bergen is one of the most convenient ways to reach the region. The journey takes about **2 to 3 hours** by car, depending on the exact location you're heading to. The most common route is via the **E16 highway**, which offers stunning views along the way.

- **What to Expect**: On the drive, you will pass through charming villages, lush landscapes, and towering mountains. The road is well-maintained, and you'll have plenty of opportunities to stop and enjoy the scenery.

By Bus

Several buses operate between Bergen and Hardangerfjord, providing an affordable and scenic way to travel. The bus ride takes about **3 to 4 hours**, with routes that pass through beautiful valleys, forests, and fjord views.

- **What to Expect**: The bus ride offers a comfortable way to enjoy the landscapes without the need to drive yourself. Some bus services offer guided tours, where you can learn about the area and its history as you travel.

By Boat

From Bergen, you can take a **boat or ferry** to Hardangerfjord. This is a great way to explore the fjord, as you'll be able to see the magnificent scenery from the water. The ferry ride typically takes around **2 hours** and operates year-round.

- **What to Expect**: A boat ride through Hardangerfjord will allow you to take in the views of waterfalls, islands, and snow-capped peaks. Some boat tours also stop at villages along the fjord, giving you the chance to explore on land.

Costs of Visiting Hardangerfjord

The cost of visiting Hardangerfjord can vary depending on the activities and experiences you choose. Here's a general breakdown:

- **Boat tours**: Prices range from **NOK 300 to NOK 1,000**, depending on the tour type.
- **Hiking**: Free, though guided hikes may cost **NOK 200 to NOK 400**.
- **Fruit picking**: Costs vary depending on the farm, typically **NOK 100 to NOK 300** for a guided tour or picking experience.
- **Museums and cultural sites**: Entrance fees generally range from **NOK 50 to NOK 200**.

Hardangerfjord is a true Norwegian gem that offers an unforgettable blend of stunning natural beauty, vibrant orchards, and rich cultural heritage. Whether you're hiking through mountains, cruising along the fjord, or immersing yourself in local traditions, there is something for everyone to enjoy in this picturesque region. Hardangerfjord promises to be a highlight of any Norwegian adventure, with its striking landscapes, charming villages, and abundant fruit harvests providing an experience like no other. Don't miss the opportunity to explore the "Orchard of Norway" and make lasting memories in one of the country's most beautiful regions.

Guided Fjord Tours

One of the most captivating ways to experience Norway's awe-inspiring fjords is through a **guided fjord tour**. These tours provide not only the opportunity to witness breathtaking landscapes but also insightful commentary about the history, culture, and geology of the region. Whether you're seeking a leisurely boat ride, an adventurous kayak trip, or a combination of both, a guided fjord tour offers a unique and immersive experience. This detailed guide will cover everything you need to know about guided fjord tours, including what to expect, what makes them special, and how to make the most of your journey through Norway's majestic fjords.

Types of Guided Fjord Tours

Fjord tours come in many forms, each offering a different perspective of the fjords and catering to different preferences and levels of adventure. Here's a look at the most popular types of guided fjord tours:

Boat Cruises

Boat cruises are the most traditional way to experience Norway's fjords. These tours typically range from a couple of hours to an entire day, with some offering overnight stays on the boat for a more relaxed and scenic experience.

- **What to Expect**: A comfortable, large boat with indoor seating and outdoor decks where you can take in the views. On board, you'll have a guide who will provide information about the fjords, the surrounding landscapes, and the villages you pass. Boat cruises are generally smooth and offer ample opportunities for photography and sightseeing. Popular boat tours include **Norway in a Nutshell**, which takes you through several of the country's most iconic fjords.

RIB (Rigid Inflatable Boat) Tours

For a more adventurous and intimate experience, a **RIB tour** offers the thrill of speeding through the fjords in a smaller, more nimble boat. These tours are perfect for those who want to experience the fjords up close and personal while feeling the excitement of a faster ride.

- **What to Expect**: RIB tours involve a smaller, open boat with a guide who leads you through narrow fjords, past waterfalls, and along towering cliffs. The ride is often faster and more exhilarating compared to a traditional boat cruise, providing you with the chance to feel the wind in your hair and get closer to the natural beauty of the fjord. Be prepared to wear a life jacket and waterproof clothing, as it can get a bit splashy!

Kayak Tours

For those seeking a more intimate and active experience, kayaking offers a unique way to explore the fjords. These guided tours provide the chance to paddle at your own pace, navigating through calm waters and getting closer to the fjord's quiet, hidden corners.

- **What to Expect**: Kayaking tours are typically small-group experiences where you'll paddle in tandem kayaks, guided by an experienced local. Your guide will share insights into the fjord's ecology, its flora and fauna, and the surrounding area. These tours are perfect for those who want a more hands-on experience and enjoy the peace of paddling through scenic waterways, often accompanied by wildlife sightings and stunning views of mountains and waterfalls.

Hiking and Fjord Combination Tours

For those who want to combine the best of both worlds, some tours offer a combination of hiking and fjord exploration. These tours typically begin with a scenic hike along the fjord's cliffs or mountainside, followed by a boat ride or kayak tour to explore the fjord's lower regions.

- **What to Expect**: This type of tour offers a physically engaging experience, where you'll get a good workout while being rewarded with panoramic views from the top. The boat or kayak portion of the tour allows you to relax and enjoy the fjord from a different perspective, all while receiving commentary from your guide about the geology, history, and cultural significance of the area.

Private Guided Tours

For a more personalized and flexible experience, **private guided tours** are a popular option. These tours allow you to tailor the journey to your own preferences, whether that means focusing on specific fjords, spending more time at certain landmarks, or adjusting the pace to suit your needs.

- **What to Expect**: On a private tour, you'll have an experienced guide to yourself or your group, offering you the freedom to ask questions, stop for photos, and explore the fjord at your own pace. Private tours can include a combination of different modes of transportation, including boats, buses, and even helicopters, to provide you with the most exclusive and personalized experience possible.

What You'll See on a Guided Fjord Tour

A guided fjord tour is designed to give you a deeper understanding of the incredible natural landscapes that Norway is famous for. The highlight of any tour is, of course, the stunning views, but there's much more to appreciate beyond the scenery. Here's what to expect along the way:

Dramatic Fjord Landscapes

Norwegian fjords are renowned for their dramatic, almost otherworldly beauty. As you embark on a guided tour, expect to witness towering cliffs, deep blue waters, and lush greenery. Some of the most iconic fjords you may explore on these tours include:

- **Geirangerfjord**: A UNESCO World Heritage site known for its steep cliffs, waterfalls like **The Seven Sisters**, and picturesque villages.
- **Sognefjord**: The longest and deepest fjord in Norway, offering a diverse landscape of glaciers, mountains, and charming coastal settlements.
- **Hardangerfjord**: Famous for its orchards, waterfalls, and vibrant villages nestled along its shores.

Waterfalls

Waterfalls are one of the most iconic features of Norway's fjords. On a guided fjord tour, you will pass by awe-inspiring waterfalls, including the famous **Vøringsfossen** or **The Seven Sisters Waterfall** in Geirangerfjord.

- **What to Expect**: As you cruise through the fjords, you'll see waterfalls cascading from high mountain cliffs into the fjord below, often surrounded by lush greenery and dramatic rock formations. Some tours allow you to get up close to these waterfalls, making for a thrilling and awe-inspiring experience.

Fjordside Villages

Many fjords are lined with quaint, charming villages that seem to have been frozen in time. A guided tour offers a great opportunity to stop at these villages and experience the local culture. Expect to see picturesque wooden houses, small harbors, and cozy cafes where you can sample traditional Norwegian foods.

- **What to Expect**: Villages like **Flåm** in Sognefjord and **Undredal** in Aurlandsfjord are must-visit spots, where you can learn about local traditions, sample fresh local produce, and enjoy the serene ambiance.

Wildlife

While on a guided fjord tour, you may also be lucky enough to spot wildlife, including seabirds, seals, and, if you're fortunate, dolphins or whales. Many tour guides will point out the local wildlife and explain their role in the fjord ecosystem.

- **What to Expect**: As you cruise along the water, keep your eyes peeled for seals basking on rocks, eagles soaring above, or pods of dolphins swimming in the waters. Some tours also offer special wildlife-focused experiences, such as whale-watching tours, where the chances of seeing larger marine animals are higher.

What's Included in a Guided Fjord Tour?

Guided fjord tours typically include everything you need for a comfortable and enriching experience. While specifics can vary by tour, here are some common inclusions:

- **Transportation**: Whether you're on a boat, kayak, or bus, transportation is provided for the entirety of the tour.
- **Guide**: A knowledgeable guide will lead you through the tour, providing insights into the geography, history, and culture of the fjord region.
- **Equipment**: If your tour involves kayaking or hiking, the necessary gear (like kayaks, paddles, life jackets, or hiking poles) will be supplied.
- **Refreshments**: Some tours may include snacks, meals, or drinks, especially if the tour is more extended in duration.
- **Photography Opportunities**: Almost every fjord tour will stop at scenic spots where you can take photos. Your guide will also point out the best spots for capturing stunning shots.

Costs of Guided Fjord Tours

The cost of a guided fjord tour can vary significantly depending on the type of tour, its duration, and the inclusions. Generally, expect to pay the following:

- **Boat Cruises**: Prices can range from **NOK 400 to NOK 2,000**, depending on the tour length and type.
- **RIB Tours**: These can cost anywhere from **NOK 600 to NOK 1,500**, with shorter tours being on the lower end of the price range.
- **Kayak Tours**: Prices usually range from **NOK 500 to NOK 1,200** per person, depending on the length of the trip and the number of people.
- **Private Guided Tours**: These can be quite expensive, with costs ranging from **NOK 3,000 to NOK 10,000** or more, depending on the level of customization.

A guided fjord tour is an unforgettable way to experience the best of Norway's natural beauty. From the towering cliffs and cascading waterfalls to the charming villages and abundant wildlife, these tours offer a rich, immersive experience that brings Norway's iconic fjords to life. Whether you choose a leisurely boat cruise, an adrenaline-packed RIB tour, or a tranquil kayak excursion, a guided fjord tour will leave you with memories that last a lifetime. Make sure to bring your camera, your curiosity, and your sense of adventure!

Chapter 5. Must-Do Experiences

Hiking trails and nature walks

Mount Fløyen Trail

The **Mount Fløyen Trail** is one of Bergen's most iconic hikes, offering stunning panoramic views of the city, fjords, and surrounding mountains. Whether you're a seasoned hiker or someone looking to enjoy a gentle climb, this trail caters to all fitness levels, making it one of the most popular hiking routes in Bergen.

Trail Level: Easy to Moderate

The **Mount Fløyen Trail** is considered **easy to moderate** in difficulty, making it suitable for most hikers, including families and casual walkers. While the hike can be steeper in sections, it's not overly strenuous and can be completed comfortably by beginners with moderate fitness. The total elevation gain is about **320 meters (1,050 feet)**, and the ascent takes approximately **1 to 1.5 hours**, depending on your pace.

What to Explore

The **Mount Fløyen Trail** is packed with natural beauty, offering a variety of landscapes to explore along the way. Here's what you can expect:

Beautiful Forests and Lush Greenery

As you begin the trail, you'll be surrounded by dense Norwegian forests, filled with tall trees, moss-covered rocks, and vibrant plant life. The forest is serene and peaceful, providing a perfect escape from the hustle and bustle of the city below.

Breathtaking Views of Bergen

As you ascend the mountain, you'll be treated to gradually improving views of Bergen. From various spots along the trail, you'll get a glimpse of the city's charming rooftops, the harbor, and the fjord stretching out to the horizon.

Fløyen Summit – Spectacular Views

Once you reach the summit of **Mount Fløyen**, you're rewarded with one of the best views in Bergen. From this point, you can see the entire city, the surrounding mountains, and a beautiful view of the coastline and fjords. The viewpoint is a perfect place to pause, enjoy the scenery, and take some incredible photos.

The Fløibanen Funicular Station

At the summit, you'll find the **Fløibanen Funicular station**, which is a popular way for visitors to reach the top. It offers a fascinating contrast to the hiking experience, as the funicular provides a smooth and quick ascent, while the hike offers a more intimate and immersive experience with nature.

A Playground for Kids

The summit also features a small playground, making it an excellent destination for families with children. It's a great spot to relax and enjoy a picnic with a view.

Hiking Paths Around the Summit

Once at the top, there are several additional hiking trails that branch out from the summit, allowing you to explore other parts of the mountain, such as **Vidden** or **Rundemanen**. If you're up for more adventure, these trails lead you through more stunning landscapes.

What to Expect

The **Mount Fløyen Trail** offers a range of sensory experiences as you hike:

- **Nature**: Lush forests, scenic meadows, and tranquil waters around the summit.
- **Wildlife**: While the trail is popular, you may still catch glimpses of local wildlife, such as squirrels, birds, and the occasional deer.
- **Weather**: The weather in Bergen can be unpredictable, so be prepared for sudden changes. Bring layers, waterproof clothing, and sturdy hiking shoes to stay comfortable.
- **Difficulty**: The trail is relatively easy, but there are some steeper sections that might challenge beginners. However, the overall ascent is manageable for most hikers.

How to Get There

Getting to the **Mount Fløyen Trail** is straightforward and accessible from Bergen city center.

By Foot:

If you're staying in central Bergen, you can easily walk to the trailhead from the city center. The hike starts from **Fløybanen Funicular Station**, located at **Vetrlidsallmenningen**, just a short walk from **Bryggen** and the city center. The walk from the city to the base of the trail takes about **10–15 minutes**.

By Funicular (Fløibanen):

While the hike itself is enjoyable, if you're looking for a less physically demanding option, you can take the **Fløibanen Funicular** up to the summit. The funicular station at the base of the mountain is easily accessible and provides a quick, scenic ride up. The journey takes only **5-8 minutes**, and you can choose to hike down or simply enjoy the view from the top.

By Bus or Car:

If you prefer to drive or take public transportation, there are buses that connect central Bergen to Mount Fløyen. However, walking from the city center is by far the most scenic and enjoyable route.

Cost

Free Hiking:

The **Mount Fløyen Trail** itself is completely **free** to hike. You can embark on the trail at your own pace without any cost, making it an excellent option for budget travelers.

Fløibanen Funicular (Optional):

If you choose to ride the **Fløibanen Funicular** instead of hiking, there is a fee. Prices for a round-trip ticket on the funicular are as follows:

- **Adults**: NOK **130** (Round trip)
- **Children (4-15 years)**: NOK **50** (Round trip)
- **Children under 4**: Free

These prices are subject to change, so it's a good idea to check current prices before your visit.

The **Mount Fløyen Trail** is a must-do hike for anyone visiting Bergen. Offering spectacular views of the city, the fjord, and surrounding mountains, the trail is a perfect way to experience Norway's natural beauty. Whether you choose to hike or take the funicular, the summit offers something for everyone: peaceful nature, invigorating hikes, and incredible panoramic vistas. It's an easy, family-friendly, and accessible adventure that provides one of the best ways to connect with the magnificent landscape of Bergen.

Mount Ulriken Trail

The **Mount Ulriken Trail** offers a more challenging and exhilarating hiking experience compared to the Mount Fløyen Trail, but it rewards hikers with stunning panoramic views, dramatic landscapes, and a true taste of Bergen's natural beauty. It's the perfect trail for those seeking a more demanding hike while still enjoying the picturesque beauty of Norway's outdoors.

Trail Level: Moderate to Hard

The **Mount Ulriken Trail** is rated as **moderate to hard** in difficulty. This hike is steeper and longer than the Mount Fløyen Trail, making it more suitable for experienced hikers or those with good fitness levels. The trail spans about **4.5 kilometers (2.8 miles)** one way, with an elevation gain of **800 meters (2,625 feet)**, so it involves some challenging ascents. On average, the hike takes between **2 to 3 hours** to complete, depending on your pace and fitness level.

What to Explore

As you make your way up the **Mount Ulriken Trail**, here are the highlights you can expect to explore:

Rugged Terrain and Scenic Forests

The hike begins in the **Løvstakken** area and moves through lush forests filled with typical Norwegian flora. As you climb higher, you'll encounter rocky terrain, small streams, and moss-covered boulders, which all contribute to the trail's wild and untamed beauty. This rugged landscape is perfect for those who love nature in its rawest form.

The Spectacular Views

One of the most rewarding aspects of hiking the **Mount Ulriken Trail** is the views that unfold as you ascend. From various spots along the trail, you'll get sweeping vistas of Bergen city, the harbor, and the surrounding fjords. On a clear day, you can even see the distant mountains and the coastline stretching far beyond Bergen.

The Summit of Mount Ulriken

At the summit of **Mount Ulriken**, you'll be treated to some of the most breathtaking panoramic views of Bergen and the surrounding areas. The top of the mountain offers views of the **Sognefjord**, the **Hardangerfjord**, and several smaller mountains that define Bergen's striking landscape. The summit itself is a popular spot for hikers to relax, enjoy a packed lunch, and take in the views.

Ulriken643 (Cable Car)

At the summit, you'll find **Ulriken643**, a cable car that offers a quicker, more leisurely way to the top. While hiking is the preferred option for adventurers, those who wish to avoid the strenuous climb can take the cable car up and hike down. The cable car provides stunning aerial views of the surrounding mountains and Bergen's cityscape.

Wildlife

Throughout the hike, you may encounter local wildlife, including birds, squirrels, and even the occasional deer. Keep your eyes peeled for some of Norway's wildlife as you traverse the trail.

Peak to Peak Hike (Optional Extension)

For experienced hikers, there is an option to extend your hike from **Mount Ulriken** to **Mount Fløyen** via the **Vidden Trail**. This challenging trek covers about **13 kilometers (8 miles)** and takes roughly **5 to 6 hours** to complete. It connects the summits of both Mount Ulriken and Mount Fløyen, offering even more jaw-dropping views and a truly memorable adventure for those seeking a full-day experience.

What to Expect

The **Mount Ulriken Trail** is an invigorating and sometimes physically demanding hike. Here's what you can expect:

- **Varied Terrain**: The trail includes both rocky and forested sections, with parts of the trail being steep and uneven. It's important to wear sturdy hiking boots to navigate the rugged terrain.
- **Sweeping Views**: As you climb, the views get better and better, with each step bringing you closer to the summit where the views of the city, fjords, and mountains are simply stunning.
- **Wild Nature**: The trail is surrounded by nature, providing an opportunity to experience Norway's landscapes at their finest, with little interference from the hustle and bustle of the city.
- **Weather Conditions**: Due to Bergen's weather, it's a good idea to bring layers, waterproof clothing, and appropriate gear. The weather can change quickly, especially at higher altitudes, so be prepared for cooler temperatures at the top even during warmer months.
- **Fitness Level**: This trail is a bit more strenuous than Mount Fløyen, so a decent fitness level is recommended. It's important to take breaks when necessary and stay hydrated, especially on warmer days.

How to Get There

The **Mount Ulriken Trail** is easily accessible from central Bergen, and here's how to get there:

By Foot:

The hike starts from the **Ulriken Cable Car Station**, which is located about **5 kilometers (3 miles)** from Bergen's city center. The walk from the city center to the base of the trail will take approximately **30 minutes**. The station is located near **Haukeland University Hospital**, so you can use public transport or walk through the city to reach it.

By Bus:

If you prefer not to walk, there are buses from the city center that take you to the **Ulriken Cable Car Station**. Bus routes **20** and **21** from Bergen city center will take you close to the trailhead, where you can start your hike. The bus ride typically takes **15-20 minutes**.

By Cable Car (Ulriken643):

If you're not up for the hike, you can take the **Ulriken643 cable car** up to the summit of Mount Ulriken. The cable car operates year-round and provides an easy and scenic way to enjoy the stunning views without the physical exertion of hiking. You can take the cable car from the base to the summit in about **8 minutes**.

Cost

Hiking (Free)

Hiking the **Mount Ulriken Trail** itself is completely **free**. The trail is open year-round, and no permits or fees are required to access it. This makes it an excellent option for budget-conscious travelers.

Ulriken643 (Cable Car)

If you decide to use the **Ulriken643 cable car** to reach the summit, here are the ticket prices:

- **Adults**: NOK **230** (Round trip)
- **Children (4–15 years)**: NOK **115** (Round trip)
- **Children under 4**: Free
- **One-way tickets**: NOK **140** for adults, NOK **70** for children

Prices may vary based on season or special offers, so it's always good to check the current rates.

The **Mount Ulriken Trail** offers a more challenging yet highly rewarding experience for those seeking an adventure in Bergen's natural beauty. The hike takes you through rugged terrain, lush forests, and rewards you with some of the best views in the region. Whether you choose to hike the full trail or take the cable car for a more relaxed journey, the summit of Mount Ulriken provides an unforgettable experience with breathtaking vistas of the city, fjords, and mountains. It's the perfect hike for those looking to immerse themselves in Bergen's wild landscapes and enjoy a true outdoor adventure.

Vidden Trail (Fløyen to Ulriken)

The **Vidden Trail**, which stretches from **Mount Fløyen to Mount Ulriken**, is one of the most popular and scenic hiking routes in Bergen. This trail offers hikers a full-day adventure through diverse landscapes, with panoramic views of the city, fjords, mountains, and forests. It's an unforgettable experience for nature lovers and outdoor enthusiasts, as it showcases the best of Bergen's natural beauty in a challenging yet rewarding hike.

Trail Level: Moderate to Hard

The **Vidden Trail** is considered **moderate to hard** in difficulty, primarily due to the distance (about **13 kilometers / 8 miles**) and the varying terrain. This is a longer hike compared to the Mount Fløyen or Mount Ulriken Trails, with an elevation gain of about **600 meters (1,968 feet)**. On average, the hike takes between **5 to 6 hours** to complete, depending on your pace and the number of breaks you take along the way. It's recommended for experienced hikers or those in good physical condition, as it involves both steep and flat sections.

What to Explore

As you embark on the **Vidden Trail**, you will pass through several breathtaking landscapes and discover incredible views and hidden gems:

Mount Fløyen – The Starting Point

Your journey begins at **Mount Fløyen**, where you can take in panoramic views of Bergen and its surrounding islands, fjords, and mountains. From this vantage point, you'll get a perfect view of the **Sognefjord** and **Hardangerfjord**, and you can enjoy the lush greenery and scenic beauty that Bergen offers.

Rolling Hills and Rocky Terrain

As you leave Fløyen behind, the trail takes you through vast, rolling hills covered in heather, moss, and grasses. The path is relatively flat at first, but soon you'll encounter sections with uneven, rocky ground that requires careful footing. The trail's varied terrain gives it an adventurous feel while offering ever-changing views.

Bergen's Cityscape and Fjords

Throughout the hike, you will be treated to spectacular vistas of **Bergen's cityscape**, which sits nestled between its mountains and harbors. The distant mountains create a dramatic backdrop for the city, while the fjords stretch far beyond the horizon. If you're lucky, you may catch glimpses of local wildlife, such as birds and deer, along the trail.

Ulriken – The Summit

The final leg of the trail takes you to **Mount Ulriken**, the highest of the seven mountains surrounding Bergen. Once you reach the summit, you'll be rewarded with magnificent 360-degree views of Bergen, the fjords, the coastline, and other surrounding mountains. The summit provides a perfect spot for a well-deserved break, with opportunities for taking photos and enjoying the sweeping views.

The Ulriken643 Cable Car

Upon reaching **Mount Ulriken**, you have the option to take the **Ulriken643 cable car** back down to the city if you prefer not to hike back. The cable car offers stunning aerial views of Bergen, and it's a fantastic way to cap off your hike.

What to Expect

The **Vidden Trail** is a rewarding, albeit demanding hike. Here's what you can expect during your adventure:

- **Varied Terrain**: The trail covers a range of terrains, from rocky and uneven paths to grassy and marshy stretches. Be prepared to cross sections with different difficulty levels, requiring careful footing at times.
- **Longer Duration**: Since the trail is approximately 13 kilometers long, you'll need to allocate at least **5 to 6 hours** for the hike. It's best to start early in the day to ensure you have enough time to complete the hike.
- **Stunning Views**: One of the biggest rewards of the **Vidden Trail** is the endless panoramic views that unfold as you hike. Whether it's the fjords, the mountains, or the city, you will be treated to some of the best scenic views Bergen has to offer.
- **Weather Conditions**: The weather can change quickly in Bergen, so bring layers and waterproof clothing. Even in summer, temperatures can drop on the mountains, and rain is always a possibility.
- **Fitness Level**: While the hike is moderately challenging, it's best suited for those with a reasonable level of fitness. Some sections are steep, and there's a fair amount of elevation gain, so take your time and enjoy the experience.

How to Get There

The **Vidden Trail** connects two of Bergen's most popular peaks, **Mount Fløyen** and **Mount Ulriken**, making it easily accessible from the city center. Here's how to get to both trailheads:

To Start at Mount Fløyen:

- **By Foot**: If you're already in Bergen city center, you can easily walk to the **Fløibanen Funicular Station** at the base of **Mount Fløyen**. The funicular ride to the top takes only **6 minutes**, and from there, you'll begin the hike on the well-marked trail.
- **By Public Transport**: You can also take buses to the **Fløibanen Funicular Station**. Bus routes **12**, **13**, and **16** stop near the station.

To Start at Mount Ulriken:

- **By Bus**: From the city center, take bus routes **20** or **21** to the **Ulriken Cable Car Station**. The bus ride takes about **15 minutes**.
- **By Foot**: If you're up for the extra effort, you can also walk to the **Ulriken Cable Car Station** from Bergen's city center, which takes around **30 minutes**.

The Connection Between Fløyen and Ulriken:

Once you complete the **Vidden Trail**, you'll arrive at **Mount Ulriken**. From here, you can either hike back the same way to Fløyen or take the **Ulriken643 cable car** down to Bergen.

Cost

The **Vidden Trail** itself is completely free to hike, but there are some costs to consider if you plan to use public transportation or the cable car:

Public Transport (Buses)

- **Adult Bus Fare**: Approximately **NOK 35–50** for a one-way trip, depending on the route.
- **Children**: Discounted fares for children typically range from **NOK 15–25**.

Fløibanen Funicular

- **Round-trip**: NOK 100–120 for adults

- **One-way ticket**: NOK 55–65
- **Children**: Discounted tickets are available for children aged **4–15 years**.

Ulriken643 Cable Car (One-Way or Round Trip)

- **Round-trip for Adults**: NOK 230
- **One-way for Adults**: NOK 140
- **Round-trip for Children (4–15 years)**: NOK 115
- **Children under 4**: Free

The **Vidden Trail** from **Fløyen to Ulriken** is one of the most spectacular and rewarding hikes you can experience in Bergen. Offering a mix of diverse terrain, panoramic views, and a true taste of Bergen's outdoor beauty, it's a hike you'll never forget. Whether you're hiking for the challenge or simply to enjoy the stunning surroundings, this trail offers an unparalleled opportunity to experience the best of Bergen's natural landscapes. Don't forget to pack appropriately for the weather, bring plenty of water, and, most importantly, enjoy the journey!

Hakon's Hall Trail

The **Håkon's Hall Trail** offers a fantastic combination of history, culture, and scenic beauty, making it an ideal hike for those interested in exploring Bergen's royal heritage. This trail takes you to **Håkon's Hall**, one of Norway's most significant medieval structures, and offers a glimpse into the city's regal past. The walk to **Håkon's Hall** is rich in history and provides a unique experience as you delve into the roots of Bergen's role as the former capital of Norway.

Trail Level: Easy to Moderate

The **Håkon's Hall Trail** is generally considered an **easy to moderate** hike, suitable for most fitness levels. The trail is relatively short, around **2 kilometers (1.2 miles)**, and involves mostly flat terrain with only a few gentle inclines. It is a family-friendly route and can be completed in about **45 minutes to 1 hour**. The relatively short distance and manageable elevation make it an excellent option for those looking for a historical walking tour rather than a strenuous hike.

What to Explore

As you embark on the **Håkon's Hall Trail**, you will encounter several points of interest, including both historical and natural features that make this trail special:

Start at Bergen's City Center

The trail begins in the heart of Bergen, and as you leave the city center, you'll pass through narrow cobblestone streets and charming alleyways that evoke the city's rich past. The walk offers an opportunity to observe the blend of modern-day life and historic architecture as you make your way towards the iconic **Håkon's Hall**.

Bergenhus Fortress

One of the highlights of the **Håkon's Hall Trail** is a visit to the **Bergenhus Fortress**, a military stronghold dating back to the 13th century. As you approach the fortress, you will see well-preserved medieval structures, including **King Håkon's Tower** and the impressive fortress walls. These historic buildings set the stage for your arrival at **Håkon's Hall**, adding to the sense of stepping back in time.

Håkon's Hall

The trail culminates at **Håkon's Hall**, a majestic building dating from the early 13th century. This hall was once the royal residence of **King Håkon Håkonsson**, and it was used for royal ceremonies, banquets, and even as a royal court. The building is a testament to the medieval period, with towering stone walls and stunning architecture. Today, **Håkon's Hall** is a museum, and you can explore its grand interior, which includes royal relics, exhibitions about Norway's history, and beautiful medieval designs.

Stunning Views of the Harbor

On the way to **Håkon's Hall**, you'll also enjoy beautiful views of the **Bergen harbor**, with its bustling activity, colorful buildings, and scenic fjords. The surrounding landscape offers great photo opportunities, with the harbor providing a picturesque backdrop to the fortress and hall. This area offers an ideal spot to pause and take in the natural beauty of the region.

The Bergenhus Fortress Park

Adjacent to the fortress is the **Bergenhus Fortress Park**, a lovely green space where you can rest after your exploration. This park provides a tranquil setting with sweeping views of the sea and the city. It's an excellent place to relax, enjoy a picnic, or simply take in the peaceful surroundings before continuing your journey.

What to Expect

The **Håkon's Hall Trail** is a relatively easy and pleasant walk with a combination of historical landmarks and natural beauty. Here's what you can expect during your journey:

- **Historic Atmosphere**: The trail offers a strong sense of history, as you pass through the medieval **Bergenhus Fortress** and finally arrive at **Håkon's Hall**. The fortifications, stone walls, and royal structures make you feel like you're walking in the footsteps of kings.
- **Scenic Views**: Along the trail, you'll be treated to stunning vistas of **Bergen's harbor**, fjords, and the surrounding mountains. The panoramic views make this hike a scenic delight, perfect for photography and appreciating the natural beauty of the region.
- **Cultural Insights**: The **Håkon's Hall** itself offers an incredible cultural experience, with its historical exhibitions and the opportunity to learn about Norway's royal past. You can expect to gain insight into the medieval Norwegian monarchy and Bergen's role in the nation's history.
- **Easy Terrain**: The trail is straightforward and does not require any advanced hiking skills. It's ideal for families, casual walkers, and anyone interested in combining light exercise with historical exploration.

How to Get There

The **Håkon's Hall Trail** is located in Bergen's city center, making it easily accessible by foot from most central hotels and attractions. Here's how to reach the trailhead:

Walking from Bergen City Center:

- The easiest way to start the **Håkon's Hall Trail** is by walking from **Bergen's city center**. From **Torgalmenningen**, head towards the harbor and follow the signs to **Bergenhus Fortress**. The trail is well-marked and will guide you directly to the fortress, from which the walk to **Håkon's Hall** begins.
- The walk from **Torgalmenningen** to the fortress takes about **10-15 minutes** on foot, depending on your pace.

Public Transport:

- If you prefer not to walk, you can take **bus routes 3, 4, or 12**, which stop near **Bergenhus Fortress**. From the bus stop, it's just a short walk to the entrance of the fortress and the **Håkon's Hall Trail**.

Cost

While the **Håkon's Hall Trail** itself is free to walk, there are some costs involved if you wish to enter **Håkon's Hall** and learn more about its history. Here's what to expect:Entry to Håkon's Hall

- **Adults**: The entry fee to **Håkon's Hall** is **NOK 120–150** for adults, depending on the season.
- **Children (under 18)**: Free entry for children and young adults.
- **Senior Citizens and Students**: Discounted tickets are available, generally around **NOK 70–100**.

Public Transport

- **Bus Fare**: Bus fares within Bergen typically cost **NOK 35–50** for adults, depending on your route.
- **Children**: Children usually pay a reduced fare of **NOK 15–25**.

The **Håkon's Hall Trail** offers a fascinating journey through Bergen's medieval history, taking you from the heart of the city to one of its most iconic landmarks. Whether you're an avid history buff or simply someone who enjoys walking through beautiful settings, this trail offers a rich cultural experience and an opportunity to learn more about Norway's royal past. From **Bergenhus Fortress** to the grand halls of **Håkon's Hall**, you'll be immersed in the region's historical legacy, while also enjoying the stunning harbor views and peaceful park surroundings. This is a must-see for anyone visiting Bergen, providing a unique way to connect with the city's rich cultural heritage.

Seafood dining: Bergen's culinary highlights

Bryggen Tracteursted

What to Expect:

Located in the historic **Bryggen Wharf**, **Bryggen Tracteursted** offers a rustic yet elegant dining experience, combining traditional Norwegian flavors with contemporary twists. The restaurant features a cozy, intimate atmosphere with wooden beams and a charming old-world vibe. Expect a menu filled with local seafood, including **fresh fish, shellfish, and traditional dishes** like **klippfisk** (salted cod), as well as regional specialties like **Lutefisk** and **fresh salmon**. The restaurant also emphasizes locally sourced, seasonal ingredients, making it a perfect representation of Bergen's culinary heritage.

How to Get There:

- **Walking**: Located in the heart of the historic **Bryggen** area, **Bryggen Tracteursted** is easily accessible on foot from **Bergen's city center**. The restaurant is within walking distance of the **Fish Market (Fisketorget)**, just a **5-minute walk**.
- **Public Transport**: You can take a bus to **Bryggen**, with routes that pass nearby. The bus stop is **Bryggen** (bus routes 3, 4, 12).

Cost:

- **Main Courses**: Prices range from **NOK 200 to NOK 400** for main seafood dishes.
- **Lunch Specials**: Expect to pay around **NOK 150 to NOK 250** for lunch options.
- **Drinks**: Alcoholic beverages such as wine and beer are available, with prices averaging **NOK 90 to NOK 150** per glass.

Fish Market (Fisketorget)
What to Expect:

The **Fish Market (Fisketorget)** is an iconic landmark in Bergen, offering a lively and bustling atmosphere where you can experience a wide range of seafood. The market itself is an open-air space where fresh fish, shellfish, and other seafood delights are sold directly from local fishermen. The seafood stalls feature **crab, lobster, shrimp, scallops, salmon**, and **cod**. You can also enjoy freshly prepared seafood dishes at the market's food stalls, including **fish soup, fish burgers**, and **sushi**. The market is a perfect place to sample fresh seafood while enjoying the lively atmosphere of Bergen's harbor.

How to Get There:

- **Walking**: The **Fish Market** is located in the **city center**, within a **5-minute walk** from the **Bryggen** and the **harbor**.
- **Public Transport**: Buses to **Fisketorget** can be accessed from nearby stops, with several bus routes passing through the central area.

Cost:

- **Fresh Fish and Shellfish**: Prices vary depending on the catch of the day, but expect to pay around **NOK 150 to NOK 350** for seafood.
- **Prepared Seafood Dishes**: Prices for cooked seafood dishes and snacks range from **NOK 100 to NOK 200**.
- **Drinks**: Soft drinks, beer, and wine are available, with prices ranging from **NOK 40 to NOK 100**.

Lysverket
What to Expect:

Lysverket is one of Bergen's top modern seafood restaurants, located by the waterfront with stunning views of the harbor. It combines innovative cooking techniques with fresh, locally sourced ingredients to create sophisticated dishes with a focus on Norwegian seafood. Expect a seasonal menu featuring a variety of fish like **mackerel**, **cod**, and **herring**, as well as an assortment of **smoked fish**, **seafood stews**, and **shellfish platters**. The restaurant offers a tasting menu for those looking for a curated culinary experience. With an emphasis on fine dining, **Lysverket** also pairs each dish with an excellent selection of wines from local vineyards and global regions.

How to Get There:

- **Walking**: **Lysverket** is located by the water at **Kjøttbasaren** in central Bergen, a **5-minute walk** from the **Fish Market** and the **Bryggen** area.
- **Public Transport**: Bus routes 3, 4, and 12 pass near **Lysverket**, and the closest bus stop is **Fisketorget**.

Cost:

- **Main Courses**: Expect to pay around **NOK 250 to NOK 450** for a main course.
- **Tasting Menu**: The tasting menu is priced at around **NOK 600 to NOK 1,000** per person.
- **Drinks**: Wine pairings typically range from **NOK 120 to NOK 250** per glass.

Cornelius Seafood Restaurant
What to Expect:

For a truly unique and luxurious seafood experience, **Cornelius Seafood Restaurant** is located on a small island just off the coast of Bergen, accessible only by boat. The restaurant is known for its **elegant setting**, fantastic views, and exceptional seafood dishes, including **lobster**, **scallops**, **fresh fish**, and a signature **seafood platter**. The menu changes based on what's freshly caught that day, making each visit a new experience. The ambiance is upscale, with floor-to-ceiling windows offering stunning views of the surrounding fjords. **Cornelius** also provides a memorable boat ride to the restaurant, which adds to the charm of the experience.

How to Get There:

- **Boat**: The restaurant offers a regular boat service from the **Bryggen harbor** in central Bergen. The boat ride takes around **30 minutes** and is included in the cost of your meal. Boats typically depart several times a day.

- **Public Transport**: You can take a bus to **Bryggen** (routes 3, 4, 12) and walk to the boat departure point.

Cost:

- **Main Courses**: Expect to pay between **NOK 350 to NOK 600** for main seafood dishes.
- **Seafood Platters**: The seafood platters range from **NOK 600 to NOK 900** per person.
- **Boat Ride**: The boat ride is included in the cost of the meal but may range from **NOK 100 to NOK 250** depending on the season and booking.
- **Drinks**: Wine and cocktails are available, typically costing **NOK 90 to NOK 150** per glass.

Each of these venues offers a different yet unforgettable way to experience Bergen's rich seafood culture, from bustling markets to fine dining with breathtaking views. Whether you're looking for a quick seafood snack or a luxurious dining experience, Bergen's seafood dining scene has something for every palate and budget.

Local markets and crafts

Bergen, often referred to as the "Gateway to the Fjords," is a city rich in history, culture, and artisanal craftsmanship. Its markets and craft scenes are a reflection of the city's heritage, offering visitors a chance to experience the creativity and traditional Norwegian culture that have been passed down through generations. From colorful stalls showcasing locally made crafts to bustling food markets filled with fresh regional produce, Bergen provides a wide variety of market experiences that will captivate any visitor.

The Fish Market (Fisketorget)

Overview: As one of Bergen's most iconic landmarks, the **Fish Market (Fisketorget)** is a must-visit for any traveler interested in experiencing the local culture. Located right by the harbor, Fisketorget is a bustling, open-air market that dates back to the 1200s, making it one of the oldest markets in Norway. Today, it remains a central hub for locals and visitors alike, offering an extensive selection of fresh seafood, regional produce, and Norwegian specialties.

What to Expect: The Fish Market is home to various seafood stalls where you can find freshly caught fish, shellfish, and other ocean delicacies like **shrimp, crab, lobster, mussels**, and **scallops**. You can also enjoy freshly prepared seafood dishes at food stalls, such as **fish soups, fish sandwiches**, and **fish burgers**. In addition to seafood, there are plenty of stalls selling locally sourced produce, Norwegian cheeses, spices, and artisan products.

Visitors to the market can also find crafts made by local artisans, from knitted wool garments and scarves to intricate woodwork and jewelry, perfect for a unique souvenir to remember Bergen by.

How to Get There:

- **Walking**: The Fish Market is located in **central Bergen**, just a **5-minute walk** from the **Bryggen** and the **harbor**.
- **Public Transport**: You can take buses that pass through the central area. The closest bus stop is **Fisketorget**.

Cost:

- **Seafood**: The price of fresh seafood varies, but expect to pay around **NOK 150 to NOK 350** for the freshest catches.
- **Prepared Seafood Dishes**: These can range from **NOK 100 to NOK 200** depending on the dish.
- **Crafts and Souvenirs**: Prices for handmade goods vary, with wool items starting at around **NOK 150**, jewelry at **NOK 200 to NOK 500**, and intricate woodwork often ranging from **NOK 250 to NOK 600**.

The Bergenhus Craft Market

Overview: The **Bergenhus Craft Market** is an excellent spot to immerse yourself in the local craftsmanship of Bergen. This market, which operates seasonally, offers a broad range of handmade goods from talented Norwegian artisans. It's a place to find unique, one-of-a-kind products that reflect Bergen's cultural heritage.

What to Expect: At the Bergenhus Craft Market, visitors can expect to find beautiful, handcrafted items such as **wooden figurines**, **handmade pottery**, **ceramics**, **textile products**, and **traditional Norwegian sweaters** (often crafted from **wool**). The market is a wonderful place to pick up artisanal home goods, decorative pieces, and clothing items, all crafted by local artists. Many of the products reflect Norway's deep-rooted traditions, often incorporating natural materials like wood, stone, and wool.

How to Get There:

- **Walking:** The market is located near **Bergenhus Fortress**, and is easily accessible by foot from **Bryggen** and **the city center**.
- **Public Transport:** Buses and trams run regularly through the city center, with **Bergenhus** being the nearest stop.

Cost:

- **Crafts:** Prices for handmade items vary, but small items like **jewelry** can cost around **NOK 150 to NOK 500**, while larger handcrafted pieces, like **wooden furniture** or **handwoven rugs**, can range from **NOK 500 to NOK 2,000**.

The Lille Lungegårdsvann Market

Overview: The **Lille Lungegårdsvann Market** is an annual arts and crafts market held in **Lille Lungegårdsvann Park**. This market celebrates Bergen's craft culture and gives visitors the chance to explore unique art pieces, designs, and handicrafts. It's an excellent venue for finding contemporary arts and crafts made by local artists, as well as traditional items that highlight Norway's history.

What to Expect: At the Lille Lungegårdsvann Market, expect to find a variety of products, including **modern artwork**, **ceramic sculptures**, **hand-painted textiles**, **knitted wool items**, and **artisan jewelry**. The market also features live demonstrations of artists working, so visitors can learn about the creative processes behind their favorite crafts. Whether you are looking for high-end art pieces, small handcrafted gifts, or home decorations, this market offers something for everyone.

How to Get There:

- **Walking: Lille Lungegårdsvann** is a central location in Bergen, easily accessible by foot from the **city center**.
- **Public Transport:** Bus routes 3, 4, and 12 stop nearby.

Cost:

- **Crafts:** Prices for items range from **NOK 50 for small trinkets** to NOK 1,000 for larger art pieces.
- **Artworks:** Larger paintings or sculptures can cost anywhere from **NOK 500 to NOK 5,000**, depending on the artist and size.

The Bryggen Craft Shops

Overview: In the heart of Bergen's **Bryggen Wharf**, a UNESCO World Heritage site, you will find a variety of shops offering traditional Norwegian crafts. The craft shops along **Bryggen** specialize in **handwoven textiles**, **wood carvings**, **leather goods**, and **knitted products**, all made using local materials. Shopping here is an opportunity to take home a piece of Bergen's history and culture, as many of the crafts are inspired by centuries-old traditions.

What to Expect: The shops offer items such as **traditional Norwegian sweaters, rosemaling (decorative painting), hand-carved wooden items, leather bags,** and **jewelry**. The vibrant colors of the Norwegian folk art and the natural materials used in the creations provide a perfect souvenir or gift. You can also find modern takes on traditional crafts, blending contemporary design with time-honored techniques.

How to Get There:

- **Walking:** These shops are located throughout **Bryggen Wharf**, easily reachable on foot from the **Fish Market** and **the city center**.
- **Public Transport:** Buses and trams pass near **Bryggen**, with several stops around the area.

Cost:

- **Crafts:** Small items such as **handmade cards** or **wooden spoons** can cost around **NOK 50 to NOK 300**.
- **Sweaters and Jackets:** Woolen garments range from **NOK 300 to NOK 1,500**.
- **Leather Goods:** Leather bags and wallets are priced between **NOK 300 and NOK 1,200**.

The Bergen Artisans Market
Overview: The **Bergen Artisans Market** is a seasonal market dedicated to showcasing the work of Bergen's finest artisans. Here, visitors can find a mix of **contemporary art, ceramics, jewelry,** and **handcrafted home décor**. Many of the artisans who participate in this market are Bergen locals, and they bring their craftsmanship directly to the people. The market provides an excellent opportunity to experience the best of Bergen's creative scene, and it's a great place to purchase something truly unique.

What to Expect: Expect to find a wide range of products, including **handcrafted pottery, ceramics, art prints, textiles, modern art,** and **custom-made jewelry**. The artisans often use **natural materials** and focus on sustainability, creating pieces that are both beautiful and eco-friendly. This is a great place for collectors and art enthusiasts to discover something new and authentic.

How to Get There:

- **Walking:** The **Bergen Artisans Market** is held in various locations around the city, but it is most commonly located in the **city center**. The **Lille Lungegårdsvann Park** is a frequent venue.
- **Public Transport:** Buses and trams can bring you to the city center.

Cost:

- **Handcrafted Items:** Prices range from **NOK 100 for small pieces** to **NOK 2,500 for larger art pieces**.

Bergen's markets and crafts provide an extraordinary experience for visitors, offering a chance to dive into the rich cultural heritage of Norway. From the bustling **Fish Market** with its fresh seafood and local produce to the **artisanal crafts** found at markets like the **Lille Lungegårdsvann** and **Bryggen shops**, there's something to suit every interest and budget. Whether you're looking for a unique souvenir, sampling local flavors, or admiring exquisite craftsmanship, Bergen's local markets are an essential part of the city's vibrant cultural landscape.

Northern Lights viewing tips

The **Northern Lights**, or **Aurora Borealis**, are one of nature's most spectacular phenomena, and seeing them dance across the night sky is a bucket-list experience for many travelers. Bergen, situated in Norway, is an ideal base for a chance to witness this mesmerizing display of light, especially in winter months. While the lights are often associated with far northern destinations like Tromsø, you can still spot them from Bergen if you know the right time, place, and conditions.

Here's a comprehensive guide to maximizing your chances of experiencing the Northern Lights in Bergen, with practical tips, where to go, and how to prepare for the best viewing experience.

Best Time to View the Northern Lights in Bergen

The Northern Lights are most visible during **the winter months**, between **September and March**. During this time, the nights are long, and the skies are dark, offering optimal conditions for viewing. However, there are certain factors to keep in mind:

- **Peak Season**: The best period for seeing the Northern Lights is typically between **October and March**, with **December through February** being the prime months. The long, dark nights during this time increase the chances of catching a display.
- **Avoiding Light Pollution**: The Northern Lights are best seen away from artificial lights. In Bergen, this means heading out of the city to more remote locations or areas where light pollution is minimal.
- **Solar Activity**: The Northern Lights are a result of solar winds interacting with the Earth's magnetic field. High solar activity means more intense aurora displays, so checking **solar activity forecasts** and **aurora prediction websites** can increase your chances of witnessing the phenomenon.

Check the Weather Conditions

Clear skies are crucial for optimal viewing of the Northern Lights. You can have the best aurora conditions, but if the sky is cloudy, you won't see anything. Here's what to watch for:

- **Clear Skies**: Look for weather forecasts predicting **clear, cloudless skies**. Check the weather frequently, as clouds can move in quickly in coastal regions like Bergen.
- **Cold, Dry Air**: The best time for clear skies is typically when the air is cold and dry. Warm air tends to bring clouds, while dry, crisp air increases your chances of seeing the auroras.

Ideal Locations for Viewing the Northern Lights Around Bergen

While Bergen itself is a beautiful city surrounded by mountains and fjords, light pollution from city lights can obscure the Northern Lights. For the best experience, head to darker, more secluded spots. Here are a few locations you might consider:

Mount Fløyen and Mount Ulriken

- **Mount Fløyen** and **Mount Ulriken** are both accessible by cable car or hiking. These two peaks offer stunning views of the city, and from here, you can often get a clear, unobstructed view of the skies. The high vantage points can also take you above the surrounding urban light pollution, increasing your chances of catching a glimpse of the aurora.

Hardangerfjord

- Located about 1.5 hours from Bergen by car, **Hardangerfjord** is an ideal spot for Northern Lights viewing. The fjord's remote setting, away from the city, offers a perfect dark sky with minimal light interference, ideal for spotting the Northern Lights over the serene landscape.

Grieg's House (Troldhaugen)

- Another great location for a quiet, peaceful experience is **Troldhaugen**, the home of famous Norwegian composer Edvard Grieg, located about 8 kilometers from Bergen. Here, you can enjoy the Northern Lights while also being surrounded by nature and the rich cultural history of the area.

Kjenndalsbreen Glacier

- For a truly magical experience, head toward **Kjenndalsbreen**, a glacier just outside of Bergen. The stillness and isolation of the area create an ideal environment for viewing the Northern Lights, far away from city lights.

Be Prepared for Cold Weather
Since you'll be venturing into the cold to witness the Northern Lights, it's essential to dress appropriately:

- **Layers**: Wear **thermal base layers** to keep warm, especially if you plan to stay outside for a prolonged period.
- **Waterproof Outerwear**: Bring a **waterproof jacket** and **pants** to protect yourself from wind and snow.
- **Warm Accessories**: Don't forget **gloves**, **hats**, and a **scarf**. Thermal gloves and hats are essential for comfort, as temperatures can drop below freezing.
- **Sturdy Footwear**: Wear **insulated and waterproof boots** to navigate icy trails or snow-covered paths safely.

Camera and Photography Tips
If you want to capture the Northern Lights on camera, here are some tips for getting the best shot:

- **Camera Settings**: Use a **DSLR** or **mirrorless camera** with manual controls. Set your camera to a **wide aperture** (f/2.8 to f/4), **ISO** between **800-1600**, and a **long exposure** of about **10-15 seconds**.
- **Tripod**: A sturdy **tripod** is essential for stabilizing the camera during long exposures.
- **Focus**: Focus your camera on a distant light or a star before turning off autofocus, as the Northern Lights will often be faint and hard to focus on.
- **Avoid Flash**: Flash can ruin the shot, so make sure it's turned off.
- **Time Lapse**: If you have a remote shutter or intervalometer, you can set up for a **time-lapse** to capture the motion of the auroras as they dance across the sky.

What to Expect When You See the Northern Lights
Once you've successfully found a good spot and the Northern Lights appear, here's what you can expect:

- **Colors**: The Northern Lights are typically green, but you can also see shades of **purple**, **red**, **yellow**, and **blue**. The colors depend on which gases are being excited in the Earth's atmosphere.
- **Movement**: The aurora isn't static; it moves and shifts across the sky. Sometimes it will look like a mist or fog, while other times, it may form distinct, vibrant arches or curtains that ripple and dance.
- **Intensity**: The brightness of the lights can vary. On a strong night, you may see vivid colors and patterns that seem to change by the second. On a quiet night, the display can be more subtle and faint.

Northern Lights Tour Options
If you'd prefer to leave the planning and driving to experts, you can book a **Northern Lights tour** from Bergen. Many companies offer organized trips to prime viewing locations. These tours can include:

- **Guided trips** to remote areas with little light pollution
- **Photographer guides** to help with your camera settings
- **Warm clothing and hot beverages** for a comfortable experience
- **Transportation** to reduce the hassle of driving in winter conditions

Witnessing the Northern Lights in Bergen is an unforgettable experience, and while the lights are never guaranteed, following the right steps can increase your chances of seeing this awe-inspiring natural wonder. Plan your visit for the winter months, head to areas with minimal light pollution, and be prepared for the cold. With a little bit of luck and careful planning, you'll have the chance to witness one of the most spectacular light shows on Earth—an experience that will stay with you for a lifetime.

Chapter 6. Family-Friendly Activities

Bergen Aquarium

The **Bergen Aquarium** is one of the city's most family-friendly attractions, perfect for both children and adults alike. Located on the scenic coastline of Bergen, this aquarium is a place where you can explore marine life from both the Norwegian waters and far-flung oceans, offering a fun and educational experience for visitors of all ages.

What to Expect at Bergen Aquarium

The Bergen Aquarium is much more than just an aquarium—it's an interactive and immersive experience where you can observe, learn, and even get hands-on with some of the creatures of the sea. Here's what to expect during your visit:

Marine Life Exhibits:

- The aquarium houses over **60 species** of fish and marine animals, showcasing a wide variety of local and exotic sea life. Expect to see **Atlantic cod**, **flatfish**, and **squid** from local waters, as well as more tropical species like **sea turtles**, **sharks**, and **exotic fish** from distant oceans.
- The large, **oceanic tanks** offer up-close views of **seals**, **penguins**, and **otters**, often interacting with their environment. Children and adults alike can marvel at these fascinating creatures as they swim, play, and dive in their habitats.

Interactive and Themed Zones:

- The aquarium has **themed zones** where you can discover the diverse ecosystems of the world's oceans. There are designated areas for **Norwegian waters, tropical seas,** and **Amazonian rainforests**.
- One of the main highlights is the **tropical zone**, where visitors can see vibrant coral reefs and brightly colored fish, mimicking the rich underwater worlds found in places like the Great Barrier Reef.
- The **aquarium's touch pool** gives visitors the chance to gently touch and interact with starfish, sea cucumbers, and other safe marine life under the supervision of the staff.

Educational Displays:

- The Bergen Aquarium offers a **wealth of educational exhibits** where children can learn about the importance of marine conservation, the fragility of ecosystems, and the significance of protecting our oceans. Interactive displays, signs, and educational programs ensure that both kids and adults understand the vital role marine life plays in the planet's well-being.
- There are also **feeding sessions** scheduled throughout the day, where visitors can watch staff feed the fish and learn about the animals' diets, habits, and behaviors.

Penguin and Seal Shows:

- One of the major attractions for families is the **daily penguin and seal feeding shows**, where you can observe these adorable creatures as they interact with the trainers and eat their meals. These shows are not only entertaining but also educational, as staff provide commentary on the animals' behaviors and their natural environments.

Outdoor Playground:

- The aquarium's location by the water provides ample space for visitors to enjoy the outdoors. There is an **outdoor playground** where children can burn off some energy, surrounded by beautiful coastal scenery.

Café and Gift Shop:

- After exploring the aquarium, you can relax at the **café**, which offers a selection of drinks, snacks, and light meals, perfect for refueling after a busy day of exploration.
- The aquarium also has a **gift shop** where you can pick up souvenirs such as plush sea animals, educational toys, and marine-themed keepsakes to remember your visit.

How to Get to Bergen Aquarium

Located on the edge of the picturesque Byfjorden (the Byfjord), the Bergen Aquarium is easily accessible for families visiting the city. Here are some options for getting there:

- **By Foot**: The aquarium is just a **10-15 minute walk** from the city center of Bergen, making it an ideal spot to reach if you're already staying in or near the downtown area.
- **By Bus**: If you prefer to take public transport, you can catch bus number **2, 3, or 6** from the city center. The journey takes about **10-15 minutes** and the bus stop is right by the aquarium.
- **By Car**: If you're driving, the aquarium is just a short distance from the center of Bergen. There are parking options available near the aquarium, though it may get busy during peak seasons.
- **By Taxi**: A taxi from the city center will take about **10 minutes** and is a convenient option if you have a group or family with children.

Cost of Admission

The Bergen Aquarium offers affordable entrance fees, with different prices for adults, children, and families. Prices may vary slightly depending on the season, so it's always a good idea to check in advance. Here's a general guide to the costs:

- **Adults (16 years and older)**: Approximately **NOK 220-250**.
- **Children (3-15 years)**: Approximately **NOK 130-150**.
- **Children under 3 years**: Free entry.
- **Family Ticket** (2 adults + 2 children): Approximately **NOK 650-750**.

They also offer **discounts** for groups, students, and seniors, so it's worth inquiring if you're traveling with a larger group or need a reduced-price ticket.

The Bergen Aquarium is an outstanding destination for families looking to explore marine life, learn about conservation, and have fun together. Whether you're observing the lively penguins, getting hands-on with marine creatures in the touch pool, or simply enjoying the beauty of the fjord-side setting, the aquarium offers something for everyone. Its combination of education, entertainment, and accessibility makes it one of Bergen's top family-friendly attractions.

Science Center VilVite

The **VilVite Science Center** in Bergen is a fantastic, family-friendly destination that invites visitors of all ages to explore, learn, and play through hands-on exhibits and interactive displays. A perfect spot for curious minds, the center offers a fascinating glimpse into the world of science and technology, making learning fun and engaging for everyone. Whether you're a child or an adult, VilVite's exciting, educational environment is a great way to discover the wonders of science in a playful and immersive way.

What to Expect at Science Center VilVite

VilVite Science Center is designed to bring science to life through interactive exhibits, experimental demonstrations, and fun activities. Here's what you can expect during your visit:

Hands-on Exhibits:

- The center features over **50 interactive exhibits** across several themed areas, covering topics ranging from physics and technology to biology, space, and the environment. You'll be able to explore **mechanical puzzles, light and sound experiments, robotics**, and much more.
- Visitors can experience activities like **building a rocket, testing the laws of physics**, or even **operating a giant bubble machine**. It's an ideal way for kids to get a deeper understanding of how the world works through firsthand exploration.

Themed Areas:

VilVite is divided into several exciting themed areas, each designed to introduce visitors to different scientific principles. Some of the key themes include:

- **The Human Body**: Explore how your body functions, how you perceive the world, and test your senses through interactive displays.
- **Technology and Innovation**: Dive into the fascinating world of technology, where you can interact with gadgets, learn about robotics, and experiment with computers.
- **Energy**: Investigate how we harness energy from different sources and understand concepts like **solar energy, wind power**, and **electricity**.
- **Physics**: Play with **kinetic energy** and **motion experiments**, discover **force and gravity**, and test your knowledge of the fundamental laws of physics.
- **Space Exploration**: Take a journey into outer space and learn about stars, planets, and the universe with hands-on space exhibits.

Temporary Exhibitions:

- VilVite frequently hosts **temporary exhibitions** that change throughout the year, covering a wide range of science-related topics. These exhibitions bring fresh perspectives on scientific concepts and often feature collaboration with universities, research institutions, and tech companies. Previous exhibitions have focused on themes like **sustainable cities, future technology**, and **space travel**.

Live Demonstrations:

- The center organizes **live science shows and demonstrations**, where you can witness science in action. These shows might include demonstrations of **chemical reactions, explosions**, or even **air pressure experiments**, engaging visitors with fun and exciting ways to learn about science.

Workshops and Activities for Children:

- VilVite offers a variety of **workshops and activities** for children, where they can engage with science in a creative, hands-on way. Workshops might include building **simple machines**, creating **electric circuits**, or even **making slime**—activities designed to spark kids' imaginations while teaching them core scientific concepts.

Learning Spaces for Schools and Groups:

- The center also caters to school groups, providing special **guided tours** and educational programs tailored to specific age groups and subjects. These programs ensure that kids not only have fun but also walk away with a deeper understanding of scientific principles.

VilVite Café and Shop:

- After exploring the exhibits, visitors can relax at the **VilVite Café**, which offers a selection of drinks, snacks, and light meals, perfect for a break during your visit. The café also provides a comfortable place to sit and discuss the exhibits you've just seen.
- The **VilVite Gift Shop** offers science-themed souvenirs, educational toys, books, and fun gadgets for both kids and adults. It's a great place to pick up a keepsake to remember your visit by.

How to Get to Science Center VilVite

VilVite is located at **Håkonsgaten 27**, just a short distance from Bergen's city center, making it easy to access. Here's how to get there:

- **By Foot**: The center is located about a **15-minute walk** from Bryggen and the main harbor area. It's an easy stroll along the waterfront, so if you're staying in or near the city center, walking is a convenient option.
- **By Bus**: You can catch bus number **4** or **5** from the city center to reach the Science Center. The bus ride typically takes around **10 minutes**.
- **By Car**: If you're driving, the center is just a few minutes from the city center. There are parking options available near the building, although they can be limited during peak tourist seasons.
- **By Taxi**: A taxi from the city center will take around **5-10 minutes** and drop you right at the entrance of the center.

Cost of Admission

VilVite Science Center offers reasonable prices for admission, and the ticket prices vary based on age and group size. The fees are generally as follows:

- **Adults (16 years and older)**: Approximately **NOK 170-190**.
- **Children (3-15 years)**: Approximately **NOK 120-140**.
- **Children under 3 years**: Free admission.
- **Family Ticket** (2 adults + 2 children): Approximately **NOK 500-550**.

VilVite also offers discounts for students, seniors, and groups. If you plan to visit multiple attractions in Bergen, you may also find packages that offer discounts when combined with other popular sites.

Why Visit VilVite?

VilVite Science Center is an essential stop for families visiting Bergen, offering a wonderful blend of education and entertainment. It provides an opportunity for families to engage with science in an interactive and playful environment, making complex topics accessible and fun. The hands-on activities, live demonstrations, and engaging exhibits create an experience that is both informative and entertaining, ensuring that everyone, from young children to adults, will leave with a deeper appreciation for the wonders of science. Whether you're looking for an educational outing or just want a fun day out with the family, VilVite is a must-see in Bergen.

Kid-friendly fjord cruises

A **fjord cruise** is one of the most magical ways to experience the natural beauty of Bergen and the surrounding areas, and it's an activity that both kids and adults can enjoy. Norway's fjords are world-renowned for their awe-inspiring landscapes, and a kid-friendly fjord cruise offers a relaxed yet adventurous way to explore these stunning natural wonders. From towering cliffs and waterfalls to peaceful waters and picturesque villages, a cruise through the fjords promises a scenic adventure that will captivate your little ones while offering adults a chance to unwind and soak in the sights.

What to Expect on a Kid-Friendly Fjord Cruise

Beautiful Views:

- A fjord cruise offers an unparalleled view of Norway's unique natural beauty. Expect to see **steep cliffs**, **snow-capped peaks**, **lush forests**, and **charming villages** nestled along the water's edge. The shimmering water and dramatic landscapes create a magical setting, making it an unforgettable experience for children and adults alike.
- Children will be mesmerized by the beauty of the fjords, especially when passing through narrow, winding waterways and getting up close to waterfalls cascading from high cliffs. Keep an eye out for wildlife, such as **seals**, **eagles**, and possibly even **whales** or **porpoises** in some areas.

Family-Friendly Boats:

- The boats on these cruises are designed to accommodate families, offering **spacious decks** where children can move around and take in the sights. Many of the larger boats have **indoor seating** and **outdoor viewing areas** to ensure comfort in varying weather conditions. There are often special areas for families with small children, making it easier to enjoy the ride without worrying about your little ones.

Guided Tours:

- On many fjord cruises, a **guided tour** is included, providing educational commentary about the **local history**, **geography**, and **wildlife** of the area. This can be a great opportunity for children to learn about the fjords and the unique ecosystems in a fun and engaging way. Guides may provide interesting facts and share stories about **Norwegian culture** and **sagas**, helping children make connections to the area's history.

Interactive Activities:

- Some cruise companies offer **kid-specific programs** on board, such as **treasure hunts**, **scavenger hunts**, or **storytelling sessions**, where children can learn more about the fjords in a fun and interactive way. These activities often include small prizes or certificates, keeping the young ones entertained while learning.
- Many of the cruises have **craft stations** or **games** to keep children engaged during the journey. These are a great way to pass the time and let kids get creative while still appreciating the incredible surroundings.

Short and Relaxed Cruise Options:

- If you're traveling with young children, you can opt for **shorter fjord cruises** that last 1.5 to 2 hours. These cruises are less strenuous and provide a relaxing outing without overwhelming little ones with a lengthy journey. The shorter trips still allow you to see the beauty of the fjords, including breathtaking views of **Norwegian landscapes**, **waterfalls**, and **quaint villages**.
- For families who prefer a longer excursion, there are also multi-hour cruises that may include additional stops at **remote villages** or include **kayaking or hiking excursions** at various points. However, most companies are mindful of family schedules, ensuring there are breaks and opportunities for stretching and moving around.

Comfort and Safety:

- Safety is a top priority on these cruises, with most boats equipped with life jackets, railings, and safety protocols. Some companies even provide children's **life jackets** to ensure that younger travelers are always safe. The crews are generally experienced in dealing with families, and many of the boats have **comfortable seating** and amenities like **restrooms** and **refreshments**.

Wildlife Spotting:

- While not guaranteed, many fjord cruises offer an opportunity to spot wildlife along the way. Kids will love the chance to spot **seals**, **dolphins**, or **sea birds**. Some cruises even feature educational sessions or video screenings about the animals and ecosystems of the fjords, providing children with an enriching learning experience.

What to Expect During the Cruise

- **Serene Waters**: As you glide through the fjords, you'll experience the calming effect of the still, mirror-like waters. Kids will love the gentle rocking of the boat and the opportunity to enjoy nature in a peaceful environment.
- **The Sound of Waterfalls**: Many cruises pass by stunning **waterfalls**, where the sound of cascading water fills the air, providing a sensory experience that is especially exciting for younger travelers. Depending on the season, you might also encounter **snowmelt waterfalls**, which are at their most spectacular during the spring months.
- **Stops Along the Way**: Depending on the tour you choose, the boat might make several stops at small **fjord villages** or **scenic viewpoints**, allowing you to explore areas of **Norwegian heritage** and **local culture**. Kids can enjoy learning about the **viking history** or marveling at how life in these remote areas has remained largely unchanged for centuries.
- **Scenic Photos**: Be sure to bring your camera, as the fjords offer **breathtaking photo opportunities**. Children will enjoy taking snapshots of their surroundings, creating lasting memories of their adventure.

How to Get There

Departure Locations:

- Most kid-friendly fjord cruises depart from Bergen's **harbor** or **Bryggen** district. These departure points are easy to access by foot from most hotels and are located in the heart of the city, so you'll have no trouble finding your way to the cruise terminal.

Booking Tickets:

- Tickets for kid-friendly fjord cruises can be booked in advance online or at the **tourist information center** in Bergen. It's recommended to book ahead during peak seasons (summer months) to ensure availability. Many cruises offer discounts for **families**, **children**, and **group bookings**.

Cost of Kid-Friendly Fjord Cruises

- **Adults**: Typically range from **NOK 350-500** for a standard 2-hour cruise.
- **Children (under 12)**: Usually around **NOK 150-250**. Some cruises offer **free admission** for younger children (under 5 years old).
- **Family Packages**: Many cruise companies offer **family packages**, where two adults and one or two children can cruise for a discounted price, around **NOK 800-1000** for a family of four.

Why Choose a Kid-Friendly Fjord Cruise?

A kid-friendly fjord cruise offers an ideal balance of natural beauty, adventure, and education for families. The cruises are designed to be engaging for young travelers, making them an excellent option for anyone visiting Bergen with children. The opportunity to witness the spectacular fjord landscapes, spot wildlife, and participate in interactive activities ensures that both kids and adults will leave the cruise with a sense of wonder and awe. It's a perfect family outing that will be cherished for years to come.

Chapter 7. Accommodation Options

Luxury hotels

Hotel Norge by Scandic

Overview: Hotel Norge by Scandic is one of Bergen's most iconic luxury hotels, offering an exceptional blend of contemporary elegance and rich history. Located in the heart of the city, this stylish hotel features modern amenities combined with the charm of Bergen's vibrant cultural scene. Whether you're visiting for business or pleasure, Hotel Norge offers a high-end experience with breathtaking views of the city and surrounding landscapes.

What to Expect:

- **Stylish Rooms**: The rooms are spacious, beautifully designed, and equipped with top-notch amenities such as flat-screen TVs, luxurious linens, and high-speed internet access. Many rooms offer stunning views of the city and the picturesque fjords.
- **Dining**: The hotel has an excellent restaurant that serves delicious Scandinavian cuisine with a modern twist. Guests can enjoy meals made with fresh local ingredients in a chic, contemporary setting.
- **Wellness Facilities**: Guests have access to a well-equipped fitness center and wellness area. The hotel also has a relaxing sauna and offers various spa treatments to rejuvenate both body and mind.
- **Exclusive Lounge**: For those looking to unwind, the hotel's exclusive lounge is the perfect place to enjoy cocktails or simply relax after a day of sightseeing or business meetings.
- **Meeting & Event Spaces**: Hotel Norge offers modern conference and event facilities, ideal for both corporate and social gatherings, with state-of-the-art equipment and services.

How to Get There:

- **By Air**: The hotel is about a 25-minute drive from Bergen Airport (BGO), which is around 18 kilometers (11 miles) away. You can easily take a taxi or use the Airport Express Bus to reach the hotel.
- **By Train**: The hotel is a 10-minute walk from the Bergen Railway Station. You can also take a local tram or bus for easy access from the station.
- **By Car**: For those driving, Hotel Norge offers on-site parking, though it's recommended to book in advance due to limited availability.

Cost:

- **Rooms**: Prices typically start around **NOK 1,800-2,500** per night for a standard room. Prices vary depending on the season, room type, and any special offers available at the time of booking.
- **Family Rooms & Suites**: Larger rooms or suites can go up to **NOK 4,000** or more per night, offering additional space and luxury features.

Clarion Hotel Admiral

Overview: Clarion Hotel Admiral is another outstanding luxury hotel in Bergen, known for its prime waterfront location and breathtaking views of the harbor and Bryggen Wharf. The hotel is housed in a historic building that exudes charm and modern comfort. With its inviting atmosphere, fantastic amenities, and close proximity to many of Bergen's main attractions, this hotel offers guests a perfect blend of convenience and luxury.

What to Expect:

- **Elegant Rooms**: The rooms at Clarion Hotel Admiral are designed with comfort and style in mind. Many rooms feature floor-to-ceiling windows, offering stunning views of the harbor and Bryggen. Expect plush bedding, modern furniture, high-quality amenities, and complimentary Wi-Fi.
- **Dining**: The hotel boasts a well-regarded restaurant and bar, where you can enjoy a delicious breakfast buffet or a relaxing meal while overlooking the harbor. The restaurant serves a variety of Scandinavian and international dishes, prepared with fresh local ingredients.
- **Rooftop Bar**: For a truly unique experience, visit the hotel's rooftop bar, which provides spectacular panoramic views of Bergen's harbor, mountains, and the historic Bryggen district. It's a great place to unwind after a day of sightseeing.
- **Event Spaces**: The hotel offers excellent facilities for conferences, meetings, and events. With its picturesque location and state-of-the-art equipment, it's a popular choice for both business and social events.

How to Get There:

- **By Air**: Clarion Hotel Admiral is located about a 25-minute drive from Bergen Airport (BGO). You can easily take a taxi, airport shuttle, or the Airport Express Bus to reach the hotel.
- **By Train**: The hotel is just a 15-minute walk from Bergen Railway Station. Alternatively, you can take a tram or bus to get there in a few minutes.
- **By Car**: If you're driving, the hotel offers parking facilities (though it is advisable to reserve in advance due to limited availability).

Cost:

- **Rooms**: Standard room rates typically range from **NOK 1,400-2,200** per night, depending on the time of year and room type. Special offers and packages may also be available.
- **Suites and Premium Rooms**: For a more luxurious experience, suites can cost anywhere from **NOK 3,000 to 5,000** per night, depending on the size and view.

Both of these hotels offer exceptional service, comfort, and prime locations in Bergen, making them top choices for travelers seeking a luxurious stay in this beautiful city.

Budget-friendly stays

Citybox Bergen

Overview: Citybox Bergen is a budget-friendly, modern hotel located in the heart of Bergen, offering sleek and simple accommodations with a self-service concept. It provides a hassle-free, efficient stay for travelers looking for a comfortable, no-frills option while exploring the city. Citybox is known for its practical design, excellent location, and great value, making it ideal for budget-conscious visitors who want to experience Bergen without compromising on comfort.

What to Expect:

- **Modern Rooms**: Rooms are minimalistic and functional, designed for those who prefer simplicity without sacrificing comfort. Expect clean, comfortable beds, a flat-screen TV, a work desk, and private bathrooms. The rooms are well-lit and have a modern Scandinavian style.
- **Self-Check-In**: As part of its innovative self-service concept, Citybox offers self-check-in kiosks, allowing guests to check in quickly and without the need for front-desk interaction. This makes the hotel ideal for independent travelers.
- **24-Hour Access**: The hotel has a 24-hour lounge area, where guests can relax, access the internet, or enjoy a snack from the vending machines. There's no formal restaurant, but guests have access to coffee and light snacks throughout their stay.
- **Prime Location**: Situated in the city center, Citybox is within walking distance to major attractions such as the Bryggen Wharf, Bergen Fish Market, and Mount Fløyen.

How to Get There:

- **By Air**: The hotel is about a 25-minute drive from Bergen Airport (BGO). You can easily take a taxi or use the Airport Express Bus to reach the hotel.
- **By Train**: The hotel is located just a 5-minute walk from Bergen Railway Station, making it very accessible if you're traveling by train.
- **By Car**: Citybox offers limited parking spaces nearby, and it's advisable to book in advance, as the area can be quite busy.

Cost:

- **Rooms**: Prices typically start around **NOK 700-1,200** per night, making it an affordable choice for solo travelers, couples, or families on a budget. Prices can vary depending on the season, so it's worth checking for special offers or discounts.

P-Hotels Bergen
Overview: P-Hotels Bergen is a budget-friendly, centrally located hotel, offering a convenient and affordable stay for travelers who prioritize location and comfort without breaking the bank. This simple hotel is well-known for its friendly service, prime location near Bergen's attractions, and reasonable pricing, making it a solid choice for those visiting the city on a budget.

What to Expect:

- **Basic Rooms**: The rooms at P-Hotels Bergen are straightforward, clean, and functional. Guests can expect comfortable beds, a flat-screen TV, a desk, and an en-suite bathroom. The hotel offers a variety of room types, including single, double, and family rooms, making it suitable for different kinds of travelers.
- **Free Wi-Fi**: Complimentary Wi-Fi is available throughout the hotel, ensuring guests can stay connected during their stay.
- **Breakfast**: A simple buffet breakfast is included in the room rate, offering a selection of cereals, bread, cold cuts, and hot beverages—perfect to start the day before heading out to explore Bergen.
- **Convenient Location**: The hotel is within walking distance to popular attractions such as the Bryggen Wharf, Bergen Fish Market, and the UNESCO World Heritage Site. It's also near several shops, restaurants, and public transport links.

How to Get There:

- **By Air**: P-Hotels Bergen is around a 25-minute drive from Bergen Airport (BGO). Taxis or the Airport Express Bus can easily take you to the hotel.
- **By Train**: The hotel is a 10-minute walk from Bergen Railway Station, making it easy to reach if you're traveling by train. It's a great choice for those arriving by rail.
- **By Car**: The hotel is located in the city center, so parking options are limited. There is public parking available nearby, but it is recommended to check availability in advance or opt for public transport.

Cost:

- **Rooms**: Prices generally start from **NOK 800-1,500** per night, depending on room type and time of booking. This is a good mid-range option for travelers seeking a balance between cost and comfort.

Unique stays: Cabins and countryside lodges

Fjord Lodge Norway

Overview: Fjord Lodge Norway offers a picturesque and serene experience for travelers seeking a getaway in the Norwegian countryside, set amidst the stunning landscapes of the fjords. This unique lodge is located near the Hardangerfjord, one of Norway's most famous and breathtaking fjords. It offers both rustic charm and modern amenities, making it ideal for those looking to immerse themselves in nature without compromising comfort.

What to Expect:

- **Cabins with Scenic Views**: The Fjord Lodge consists of charming wooden cabins, each with spectacular views of the fjord and surrounding mountains. These cabins are designed to blend into the natural environment, offering guests a tranquil atmosphere. Expect to find cozy living spaces with modern interiors, fully-equipped kitchens, and spacious outdoor decks where you can enjoy the scenery.
- **Outdoor Activities**: The lodge offers a variety of activities to enjoy the surrounding natural beauty. Whether it's kayaking on the fjord, hiking through the mountains, or fishing in the pristine waters, there's something for everyone. In winter, guests can enjoy cross-country skiing and snowshoeing.
- **Sustainability**: Fjord Lodge is committed to sustainability and eco-friendly practices. The cabins are built using environmentally conscious methods, and the lodge encourages guests to minimize their environmental impact.
- **Relaxing Atmosphere**: The peaceful surroundings provide an ideal setting for relaxation. Guests can unwind in the cozy cabins, enjoy a cup of coffee on the deck, or take a leisurely walk along the fjord.

How to Get There:

- **By Air**: The nearest airport is Bergen Airport (BGO), which is approximately a 2-hour drive from the lodge. From the airport, you can rent a car or take a taxi to reach the lodge.
- **By Train**: The train station in Bergen connects to the surrounding areas, and you can take a train to a nearby station, followed by a short drive to the lodge.
- **By Car**: If you're driving, take the E16 and then follow the signs for the Hardangerfjord area. The lodge is easily accessible by car, and parking is available on-site.

Cost:

- **Cabins**: Prices for the cabins vary depending on the size and season, starting from approximately **NOK 1,200-2,500** per night. Expect higher rates during peak seasons such as summer and the holidays.

Voss Fjellandsby Cabins

Overview: Voss Fjellandsby Cabins is a beautiful mountain retreat located in the heart of the Voss region, offering a perfect escape for nature lovers, adventure seekers, and families. The cabins are nestled among the mountains, providing a peaceful and scenic location for those looking to explore the outdoors. Voss is well-known for its outdoor activities, and the cabins serve as a great base for hiking, skiing, and exploring the stunning Norwegian countryside.

What to Expect:

- **Mountain Cabins with Comfort**: The cabins at Voss Fjellandsby are cozy and well-equipped, featuring fully furnished living spaces, kitchens, and large windows offering breathtaking views of the surrounding mountains and valleys. The cabins range in size, from smaller options for couples to larger ones for families or groups.
- **Outdoor Activities**: Voss is a popular destination for outdoor activities year-round. During the summer months, guests can enjoy hiking, cycling, and rafting, while winter brings opportunities for skiing, snowboarding, and snowshoeing. Voss Fjellandsby also provides direct access to a ski resort, making it a prime location for winter sports enthusiasts.

- **Family-Friendly**: The cabins are ideal for families, with plenty of space for children to enjoy outdoor activities. The area is safe and offers many kid-friendly options, such as sledging, ice skating, and more.
- **Peaceful Setting**: Located away from the hustle and bustle of the city, the cabins offer a quiet retreat where you can unwind and reconnect with nature. The peaceful surroundings are perfect for stargazing, enjoying a cup of hot cocoa by the fire, or simply relaxing in the great outdoors.

How to Get There:

- **By Air**: The nearest airport is Bergen Airport (BGO), approximately 1.5 hours away by car. From the airport, you can rent a car or take a bus to reach Voss.
- **By Train**: Voss is well-connected by train, with direct routes from Bergen and other Norwegian cities. The train ride offers scenic views, and the station is located just a short distance from the cabins.
- **By Car**: If you're driving, Voss is accessible via the E16 highway, and there is parking available at the cabins.

Cost:

- **Cabins**: Rates for the cabins at Voss Fjellandsby start from approximately **NOK 1,000-2,500** per night, depending on the size and time of year. Prices may be higher during peak seasons like winter holidays and summer.

Chapter 8. Getting Around Bergen

Public transportation tips

Bergen, one of Norway's most charming cities, has an efficient public transportation system that can help you easily navigate the city and its surroundings. Whether you're heading to one of the fjords, exploring the city center, or going on a hiking adventure, public transportation is an affordable and convenient option. Here's everything you need to know to make the most of your time in Bergen using public transport.

Getting Around by Bus

Bergen has a well-developed bus network that connects various neighborhoods, the city center, and even outlying areas like Bergenhus and Nordnes.

What to Expect:

- **Bergen Bus Service**: The city buses are operated by Skyss, and they are reliable and run on a regular schedule. You can catch buses at various stops throughout the city, and they are typically on time.
- **Routes**: There are several routes to major attractions such as Mount Fløyen, the Bergen Aquarium, and Bryggen Wharf. Buses also provide access to surrounding areas like the fjords and nearby towns like Voss and Åsane.
- **Bus Tickets**: You can buy tickets directly from the bus driver using a contactless payment card (Visa/Mastercard) or pay by mobile through the Skyss app. It's also possible to buy single tickets or multi-ride passes.

How to Get There:

- Bus stops are clearly marked throughout Bergen, with electronic signs showing bus schedules. Popular bus stops include the Bergen Bus Terminal and the main station near the city center.

Cost:

- **Single Ride**: A single adult ticket typically costs around **NOK 38** (depending on the distance). A child ticket is usually about half the price of an adult fare.
- **Day Pass**: If you're planning to travel a lot within the city, a day pass may be the most economical choice. It costs around **NOK 100-150** for unlimited travel within Bergen for one day.

Trains for Longer Journeys

Bergen is connected to the rest of Norway via an extensive rail network. The Bergen Railway offers one of the most scenic train journeys in Europe, connecting Bergen to Oslo.

What to Expect:

- **Bergen to Oslo Train**: The train ride from Bergen to Oslo takes about **6.5 hours**, offering panoramic views of mountains, lakes, and forests along the way.
- **Local Trains**: Within Bergen, you can take the Bergen Line to nearby cities like Voss or Myrdal, where you can connect to famous scenic routes like the Flåm Railway.

How to Get There:

- **Bergen Train Station** (Bergen Stasjon) is located in the city center, easily accessible from most of the major attractions. From here, you can catch both local trains and longer-distance trains.

Cost:

- **Bergen to Oslo**: A one-way ticket on the Bergen-Oslo train route costs around **NOK 350-500** depending on how early you book and the class of service.
- **Local Train Fares**: Prices for local trains vary, but a short ride within Bergen typically costs **NOK 40-70**. Discounts are available for children and senior citizens.

Light Rail (Bybanen)

Bergen's Light Rail (Bybanen) is an excellent option for getting around the city. The light rail system connects the city center with neighborhoods like Nesttun, Lagunen, and Bergen Airport, making it an efficient option for both locals and tourists.

What to Expect:

- **Fast and Convenient**: The Bybanen is a modern tram system, fast, comfortable, and eco-friendly. It has a relatively frequent service and is an easy way to travel between downtown Bergen and more suburban areas.
- **Stops and Routes**: It runs from the city center, with stops at popular destinations like the Bergen Museum of Art and the Lagunen shopping mall. The Bybanen also connects with bus services, making it easy to continue your journey across Bergen.

How to Get There:

- **City Center**: The main starting point is at the Bergen Railway Station, where you can hop onto the tram and head towards the southern neighborhoods or the airport.
- **Ticketing**: Tickets can be purchased from vending machines at tram stops or via the Skyss app.

Cost:

- **Single Ticket**: A one-way adult ticket typically costs around **NOK 38**.
- **Day Pass**: A day pass covering both Bybanen and buses costs around **NOK 100-150**, which is ideal if you plan to explore several areas in a day.

Ferries and Boats

Bergen is famous for its coastal beauty, and ferries and boats are an excellent way to explore its scenic harbor and nearby islands.

What to Expect:

- **Harbor Ferries**: Regular ferries operate between the city center and the surrounding islands like Askøy, Loddefjord, and Sotra. These ferries are part of the public transportation network, and you can easily hop on and off to explore the area.
- **Fjord Cruises**: Bergen is also known for its fjords, and many operators run scheduled fjord cruises from the city. While these cruises are mainly tourist-focused, they're a fantastic way to experience Bergen's natural beauty from the water.

How to Get There:

- **City Center**: The ferry terminals are located in the heart of Bergen's harbor, and you can easily catch a ferry from here to nearby islands.
- **Booking**: Tickets for ferries can be purchased at the terminal or through the ferry operator's website.

Cost:

- **Island Ferries**: A one-way ticket on a regular ferry to an island like Askøy or Sotra costs about **NOK 40-80** for an adult.
- **Fjord Cruises**: For a scenic fjord cruise, expect prices to range from **NOK 200-500** depending on the length of the tour.

Taxis

While taxis are not the most budget-friendly option, they can be a good choice if you're traveling with a group, have a lot of luggage, or need a ride at odd hours.

What to Expect:

- **Convenient**: Taxis are readily available in the city center and can be booked via phone or through a taxi app. Most drivers speak English, so communication should not be an issue.
- **Fares**: Taxis in Bergen are metered, and you'll be charged based on the distance and time of day.

Cost:

- **Base Fare**: The initial fare is typically around **NOK 75-100**, with additional charges for distance traveled. A short ride within the city center can cost around **NOK 150-200**.

General Tips for Public Transportation in Bergen:

- **Plan Ahead**: Use the **Skyss app** to check schedules, routes, and ticket prices for buses, trams, and trains. This will help you plan your trip more efficiently.
- **Cashless Payments**: Most public transportation in Bergen is cashless. Be sure to have a contactless payment card or download the Skyss app on your smartphone for easy ticketing.
- **City Travel Pass**: If you plan to use public transportation frequently, consider purchasing a **Bergen City Travel Pass** for discounted fares and unlimited travel within a certain time period.

By following these tips and utilizing Bergen's public transportation network, you'll be able to easily explore the city's main attractions and natural beauty without breaking the bank.

Renting bikes or cars

Whether you're looking to pedal through Bergen's picturesque streets or take a scenic drive through the surrounding fjords and countryside, renting a bike or car gives you the freedom to explore the city and its natural beauty at your own pace. Both options come with their unique advantages, depending on your preferences and travel style.

Renting Bikes in Bergen

Biking is a fantastic way to explore Bergen, particularly if you want to enjoy the city's vibrant neighborhoods and access spots that are less accessible by foot. With a blend of urban trails and scenic routes, biking is an eco-friendly and enjoyable way to see Bergen.

What to Expect:

- **Bike Lanes and Trails**: Bergen is a bike-friendly city with designated bike lanes in many areas, especially in the city center and along popular waterfront areas. There are also scenic biking trails around the city and through nature reserves, offering views of the fjords, forests, and mountains.
- **Cycling Infrastructure**: While Bergen is surrounded by steep hills and mountains, the city center and some nearby areas offer flatter terrain, making it a relatively easy city to navigate on two wheels.
- **Bike Types**: Rental companies typically offer a range of bikes, from regular city bikes to electric bikes, which make it easier to conquer the city's hilly landscape. Mountain bikes and tandem bikes are also available for those looking to explore the outskirts or take more adventurous routes.

How to Rent a Bike:

- **Bike Rental Shops**: There are several bike rental shops located near the city center and tourist attractions like Bryggen Wharf, Mount Fløyen, and Bergen Railway Station. These shops often provide maps of bike-friendly routes and tips on where to go.
- **Public Bike Rentals**: You can also rent bikes through local bike-sharing programs such as **Bergen Bike Share**. With this service, you can easily pick up and drop off bikes at various points around the city, making it a convenient option for short trips.
- **Booking**: It's possible to rent bikes directly from rental shops on a walk-in basis, but during peak tourist seasons, it's recommended to book in advance through the shop's website or by calling ahead.

Cost:

- **Standard Bikes**: Rental fees for a standard bike usually range from **NOK 200-350 per day**. Prices can be slightly higher for electric bikes.
- **Electric Bikes**: Renting an electric bike typically costs between **NOK 400-600 per day**.
- **Bike Share Programs**: For short trips, a bike-sharing service can cost around **NOK 30-50 per hour**, with discounts for longer rentals.

What to Expect While Biking:

- **Scenic Routes**: Cycling along the Bergen waterfront offers spectacular views of the harbor and nearby mountains. There are also trails leading out to picturesque spots like the Nordnes Peninsula and the hills around Mount Fløyen.
- **Accessibility**: Although the city has some hilly areas, biking around the city center and along flat waterfront routes should be easy for most cyclists. If you prefer a more relaxed ride, you can opt for an electric bike.
- **Safety**: Bergen's bike lanes are generally safe, but it's important to be cautious when cycling along busy streets. Always wear a helmet (which is mandatory in Norway), follow traffic rules, and use hand signals when turning.

Renting Cars in Bergen

If you're planning to explore beyond Bergen's city limits or want the flexibility to visit remote fjords and charming towns at your own pace, renting a car is an excellent option. With Bergen located at the heart of Norway's fjord region, renting a car allows you to explore some of the country's most breathtaking natural landscapes, including the Hardangerfjord, Sognefjord, and the scenic routes to Ålesund and the Lofoten Islands.

What to Expect:

- **Scenic Drives**: Bergen is surrounded by magnificent natural landscapes, and renting a car gives you the freedom to drive through fjords, past mountains, and along coastal roads. Popular scenic drives include the Hardangerfjord route, the Sognefjord, and the winding roads leading to the mountainous regions of the Jotunheimen National Park.
- **Road Conditions**: Norway's roads are well-maintained and generally safe, even in winter months when they're equipped with snow tires. However, some rural roads and mountain passes can be narrow and winding, so driving in more remote areas requires extra caution. Ensure you have a GPS or map for directions, especially if traveling to unfamiliar regions.
- **Parking**: Parking in the city center of Bergen can be limited and expensive. Look for public parking lots or garages, and be aware of local parking regulations. Many accommodations offer parking facilities, so it's worth checking with your hotel or rental provider in advance.

How to Rent a Car:

- **Rental Agencies**: There are several international and local car rental companies located at Bergen Airport (Flesland) and in the city center. Major brands like Hertz, Avis, and Europcar offer a variety of rental options, from compact cars to larger vehicles for families or groups.
- **Booking**: You can book a car rental in advance through the agency's website or by contacting them directly. Renting in advance is recommended during peak travel seasons, especially if you have specific vehicle preferences.

Cost:

- **Compact Car**: A basic compact car rental typically costs around **NOK 400-600 per day**. Prices vary based on the car type, rental duration, and season.
- **Luxury or Larger Cars**: Renting a larger or luxury vehicle may cost between **NOK 800-1,500 per day**.
- **Fuel**: Gasoline prices in Norway can be high, so plan your fuel costs accordingly. The average price of petrol is around **NOK 16-20 per liter**.

What to Expect While Driving:

- **Breathtaking Views**: Driving through the fjord regions, you will be treated to some of the most stunning natural beauty in the world, including vast mountain ranges, clear blue lakes, and tranquil fjords.
- **Weather Conditions**: In winter months, expect cold temperatures, snow, and icy conditions, especially in the mountains. Make sure your rental car is equipped with winter tires, and check weather forecasts before heading out.
- **Toll Roads and Ferries**: Many roads in Norway, particularly in the fjord areas, require a toll payment. Be sure to bring a credit card, as some toll booths are automated and do not accept cash. Additionally, ferries are often used to cross fjords, and you'll need to pay for these crossings as part of your journey.

Final Tips for Renting Bikes or Cars in Bergen:

- **Plan Ahead**: Whether renting a bike or car, it's advisable to book your rental in advance, especially during peak tourist seasons, to ensure availability and better prices.
- **Consider Your Itinerary**: If you only plan to explore the city center, a bike might be the best option for you. However, if you wish to explore the wider region, a car is the better choice.
- **Check the Rental Agreement**: Ensure you read and understand the terms of the rental agreement, including insurance coverage, mileage limits, and fuel policies for car rentals.

Renting a bike or car in Bergen offers you the flexibility to explore at your own pace and enjoy the beauty of both the city and its surroundings. Whether you're biking through the scenic city streets or embarking on a driving adventure into the fjords, you'll be sure to experience Bergen in a way that's truly unforgettable.

Walking tours

Bergen, Norway, is a city best explored on foot, where every turn reveals a new story, a hidden gem, or a stunning view. With its picturesque streets, historic architecture, and breathtaking natural surroundings, walking tours allow you to immerse yourself in the city's rich culture and heritage at your own pace. Whether you're a history enthusiast, a nature lover, or simply someone who enjoys wandering through charming streets, Bergen offers walking tours for all interests.

Why Choose a Walking Tour in Bergen?

- **Intimate Exploration**: Unlike other modes of transportation, walking allows you to experience the nuances of a place up close. You'll have time to appreciate the city's beautiful details, from the colorful wooden houses of Bryggen to the intricate architecture of the old wharfs.
- **Flexibility**: Walking tours allow you to explore at your own pace. You can stop to take photos, enjoy a coffee break at a local café, or simply linger in front of a historical landmark that catches your eye.
- **Sustainable**: Exploring on foot is an environmentally friendly way to travel and helps reduce your carbon footprint. Plus, walking gives you a chance to stay fit and enjoy the fresh Norwegian air!

Types of Walking Tours in Bergen

Guided Historical Tours Bergen is a city steeped in history, and a guided historical walking tour is the best way to discover the stories behind its most famous landmarks. From the UNESCO World Heritage site of Bryggen Wharf to the medieval Bergenhus Fortress, you'll hear fascinating tales of the city's development, the Hanseatic League, and the Viking Age.

- **What to Expect**: Knowledgeable local guides share insider stories and historical insights, enriching your experience of key locations such as the old town, the fish market, and the famous wooden houses of Bryggen.
- **Duration**: Typically 1.5 to 2.5 hours.
- **Cost**: Prices range from **NOK 150-350** per person, depending on the tour length and inclusions.

Scenic Fjord Walks While Bergen is known for its vibrant urban culture, it's also surrounded by natural beauty. Scenic walking tours offer the opportunity to explore the stunning fjord landscapes, either within the city or in nearby areas like Nordnes or Mount Fløyen.

- **What to Expect**: These walks may take you along the shores of the fjord, through forested areas, or up into the hills for panoramic views of Bergen and the surrounding waters. You might pass by peaceful parks, picturesque beaches, and tranquil paths along the harbor.
- **Duration**: Typically 2-3 hours, though some tours may extend into half-day excursions.
- **Cost**: Tours range from **NOK 250-500** per person.

Food and Culture Walks For those interested in food and local culture, a culinary walking tour is a great way to experience the flavors of Bergen. These tours often take you to some of the city's best restaurants, bakeries, and markets, with tastings of Norwegian delicacies like fresh seafood, cured meats, and traditional pastries.

- **What to Expect**: A professional guide will lead you through the city's most iconic food spots, from the Fish Market to hidden eateries and cozy cafés. Along the way, you'll learn about Bergen's food traditions and the best places to enjoy the local cuisine.
- **Duration**: Approximately 3 hours.
- **Cost**: Prices typically range from **NOK 500-700** per person.

Art and Architecture Tours Bergen has a thriving arts and culture scene, and an art-focused walking tour will lead you to galleries, museums, and architectural landmarks. This tour is perfect for those who appreciate modern art, traditional Norwegian designs, and innovative architecture.

- **What to Expect**: Highlights may include stops at the Kode Art Museums, with their impressive collections of Norwegian and international art, as well as visits to the historic buildings and quirky, contemporary structures found throughout the city.
- **Duration**: Usually 2-3 hours.
- **Cost**: Around **NOK 300-500** per person.

Nature Walks and Hikes Bergen is known for its dramatic natural beauty, with its steep hills, lush forests, and mountain views. If you're looking to get out of the city center, consider joining a nature walk or guided hike. These tours often lead to Mount Fløyen, Mount Ulriken, or other nearby mountains, offering both easier trails and more challenging hikes.

- **What to Expect**: Depending on the hike, you'll be able to take in panoramic views of the city, fjords, and surrounding wilderness. You might walk through serene woodlands or along rugged ridges with stunning views over the city below.
- **Duration**: Typically 2-4 hours.
- **Cost**: Prices for guided hikes generally range from **NOK 300-600** per person.

Night Walks Explore Bergen's charms after the sun sets with a nighttime walking tour. As the city takes on a different atmosphere when the lights twinkle along the harbor and streets empty out, these tours offer a unique perspective on Bergen's beauty and history.

- **What to Expect**: Nighttime tours often focus on the more mysterious and eerie aspects of the city's history, including tales of ghosts, local legends, and the darker side of Bergen's past.
- **Duration**: Typically 1.5 to 2 hours.
- **Cost**: Around **NOK 150-300** per person.

How to Join a Walking Tour

- **Tour Companies**: Several local companies offer walking tours in Bergen. Some of the most popular ones include **Bergen Guideservice**, **Bergen Walking Tours**, and **Fjord Tours**. You can book tours in advance on their websites or at the local tourist office.
- **Private Tours**: For a more personalized experience, consider booking a private walking tour. This option is great if you want a tailored itinerary or have special interests.
- **Self-Guided Tours**: If you prefer to explore on your own, you can opt for a self-guided walking tour. Download a tour map or app and follow the route at your own pace. This option is often more affordable and flexible.

What to Bring on a Walking Tour

- **Comfortable Shoes**: Bergen's cobbled streets and hilly terrain require sturdy, comfortable footwear. Choose walking shoes or sneakers that are good for both urban exploration and nature walks.
- **Weather Gear**: The weather in Bergen can be unpredictable, so bring a lightweight waterproof jacket and layers that you can adjust depending on the temperature.
- **Water and Snacks**: Bring a bottle of water, especially for longer walks, and pack some snacks if you plan on being out for several hours.
- **Camera**: Don't forget your camera or smartphone to capture the stunning sights and memories from your walk around the city.

Bergen offers a variety of walking tours that cater to different interests and abilities, from historical strolls through the UNESCO-listed Bryggen Wharf to nature hikes in the surrounding mountains. Whether you're exploring the city's rich cultural heritage, sampling its culinary delights, or hiking through its breathtaking landscapes, walking tours provide a memorable and immersive way to experience all that Bergen has to offer.

Chapter 9. Day Trips and Nearby Adventures

Visiting Rosendal

Nestled at the heart of Norway's stunning Hardangerfjord, Rosendal is a small village that offers a peaceful retreat surrounded by majestic mountains, lush valleys, and a picturesque waterfront. Known for its historical sites, rich cultural heritage, and breathtaking natural beauty, Rosendal is the perfect destination for travelers seeking to experience the true essence of Norway's fjord landscape. Whether you're looking to explore unique landmarks, enjoy outdoor activities, or simply relax in serene surroundings, Rosendal has something to offer every visitor.

What to Explore in Rosendal

Baroniet Rosendal (Rosendal Manor) One of the most iconic attractions in Rosendal, **Baroniet Rosendal**, is a magnificent manor house built in the early 17th century. This historic estate offers a glimpse into Norwegian nobility's way of life, featuring beautifully preserved interiors, manicured gardens, and a rich history.

What to Expect:

Tour the manor's rooms, which are furnished with period pieces and historical artifacts.

Stroll through the lovely gardens, which are among the most beautiful in Norway. The lush surroundings include rare plants, trees, and well-maintained flower beds.

Learn about the history of the Baron family and how the estate has been preserved over the centuries.

Cost: Entry to the manor and gardens typically costs around **NOK 150-200** for adults, with discounts for children and seniors.

Hardangerfjord and Surrounding Landscapes Rosendal lies at the edge of **Hardangerfjord**, one of Norway's most stunning fjords, known for its deep blue waters, snow-capped peaks, and green valleys. Whether you're looking to explore by boat, hike along scenic trails, or simply relax by the water, the fjord offers an abundance of outdoor activities.

What to Expect:

Take a boat trip to explore the fjord's tranquil waters and its picturesque surroundings.

Enjoy hiking trails that offer spectacular views of the fjord and mountains. Some popular routes include the hike to **Løyning Mountain** and the **Rosendal to Skånevik** trail.

Spend time at the local beaches or picnic spots along the shore, surrounded by breathtaking scenery.

Cost: Boat tours range from **NOK 300-600** per person, depending on the length and type of the tour. Hiking trails are free to access, though guided hikes may charge a fee.

Hike to the Glacier For those looking for an active adventure, a hike to the **Folgefonna Glacier** is an unforgettable experience. The Folgefonna National Park, located just outside of Rosendal, is home to one of Norway's largest glaciers, offering stunning views of the ice fields and surrounding mountains.

What to Expect:

Hike through lush forests, past pristine lakes, and up to the glacier, where you'll witness dramatic ice formations.

The trail can be challenging but is suitable for experienced hikers.

In the summer months, it's also possible to take part in guided glacier tours, where expert guides will ensure your safety as you explore the glacier's icy surface.

Cost: Guided glacier tours typically cost around **NOK 800-1,200** per person, depending on the tour's length and difficulty.

Rosendal Church A quaint, white wooden church located in the village center, **Rosendal Church** is one of the oldest wooden churches in Norway, dating back to the 1850s. The church is beautifully preserved, with intricate woodwork and a serene atmosphere, making it a peaceful spot to reflect.

What to Expect:

The church is small but charming, with lovely stained glass windows and wooden pews.

It's a great place to learn more about the history of the region and its religious heritage.

Cost: Entry to the church is free, though donations are appreciated.

Vang Memorial Park For a quiet stroll in nature, head to **Vang Memorial Park**, a tranquil park located by the waterfront. The park features beautiful sculptures and provides stunning views of the fjord and surrounding mountains.

What to Expect:

Wander through the park's pathways, surrounded by lush greenery, flowers, and outdoor art installations.

Take in the peaceful surroundings while enjoying panoramic views of the fjord and nearby mountains.

Cost: Free to visit.

What to Expect in Rosendal

- **Tranquility**: Rosendal is a serene and peaceful village, far removed from the hustle and bustle of larger cities. The atmosphere is laid-back, making it an ideal destination for those looking to unwind in nature.
- **Natural Beauty**: The village is enveloped by stunning fjord landscapes, towering mountains, and lush forests. The scenery is breathtaking at any time of year, with each season offering its own unique charm.
- **Local Hospitality**: Rosendal is home to a welcoming community of locals who are proud of their heritage and eager to share their stories with visitors. Expect friendly encounters at restaurants, local shops, and even on hiking trails.

How to Get There

By Car: The drive to Rosendal is scenic and relatively easy to access from major cities like Bergen. From Bergen, the journey takes approximately **1.5 to 2 hours**, depending on traffic, along Route 49 through the stunning landscape of the Hardanger region.

Tip: If you're driving, consider taking the **Hardanger Bridge**, which offers fantastic views of the fjord and surrounding mountains.

By Bus: You can also reach Rosendal by bus from Bergen, with services operated by **Nor-Way Bussekspress**. The bus ride takes around **2.5 hours** and is a convenient option if you don't want to drive.

Tip: Buses are comfortable and provide scenic views during the journey. Be sure to check schedules ahead of time as bus services may be less frequent during the off-season.

By Boat: For a more scenic and leisurely journey, you can take a boat trip from Bergen to Rosendal. The boat ride takes around **3 hours** and provides a stunning view of the Hardangerfjord as you approach the village.

Tip: This is an ideal option for visitors who want to experience the fjord from the water and take in the surrounding beauty before arriving in Rosendal.

Cost of Visiting Rosendal
- **Accommodation**: Prices for accommodation in Rosendal can vary depending on the time of year and the type of lodging. Expect to pay around **NOK 800-1,500** per night for a mid-range hotel or guesthouse, while more luxurious options may cost up to **NOK 2,500** per night.
- **Dining**: Dining in Rosendal is reasonably priced. You can enjoy a meal at a local café or restaurant for around **NOK 150-300** per person, with seafood and traditional Norwegian dishes being local specialties.
- **Attractions**: Entry to the main attractions, such as Baroniet Rosendal, costs around **NOK 150-200** per adult. Guided glacier tours, hikes, and boat trips will typically cost anywhere from **NOK 300-1,200** per person.

Tips for Visiting Rosendal

- **Weather**: The weather in Rosendal can be unpredictable, so be sure to pack layers, including a waterproof jacket, sturdy shoes for hiking, and sunscreen for sunny days.
- **Timing**: The summer months (June to August) are the most popular time to visit, with long daylight hours and mild temperatures. However, spring and autumn also offer beautiful landscapes with fewer crowds.
- **Stay Active**: Take advantage of the various outdoor activities in the area, from hiking and glacier tours to fjord cruises and nature walks.
- **Local Specialties**: Don't miss out on trying local food such as **raspeballer** (Norwegian potato dumplings), fresh fish, and local berries in the summer.

Rosendal is a hidden gem in Norway, offering an idyllic escape into nature and history. Whether you're exploring its scenic fjords, visiting the historic manor house, or hiking to the Folgefonna Glacier, Rosendal promises a memorable and enriching experience.

Exploring Voss and its activities

Voss, located in the heart of Norway's fjord region, is a small town known for its incredible natural beauty, outdoor adventure opportunities, and traditional Norwegian charm. Nestled between towering mountains, deep valleys, and picturesque lakes, Voss offers a perfect mix of scenic landscapes and adrenaline-pumping activities. Whether you're a thrill-seeker, a nature enthusiast, or someone looking to immerse yourself in local culture, Voss has something special for every visitor.

What to Explore in Voss

Voss Fjord and Lake Vangsvatnet Voss is surrounded by water, and one of the best ways to experience the town is by exploring its fjord and lake. **Lake Vangsvatnet**, located right by the town center, is a serene body of water with crystal-clear views of the surrounding mountains.

What to Expect:

Enjoy a leisurely walk or bike ride around the lake, offering stunning views of the town and surrounding mountains.

You can rent kayaks or paddleboards to explore the lake more closely or take a boat tour of the Voss Fjord.

The area around the lake is a fantastic spot for a picnic or simply relaxing by the water.

Cost: Boat rentals, kayaks, and paddleboards typically cost **NOK 200-500** per hour. If you join a boat tour, the cost may range from **NOK 300-600** per person.

Voss Gondol and Mount Hanguren For spectacular views of the town and surrounding landscape, a ride on the **Voss Gondol** is a must. The gondola takes you up to **Mount Hanguren**, where panoramic views of the town, Lake Vangsvatnet, and the surrounding mountains await.

What to Expect:

Take the gondola ride to the summit of Mount Hanguren for unparalleled views of the fjord, mountains, and valleys below.

There are several hiking trails that start from the top of the gondola, allowing you to explore the area further.

In the winter, Mount Hanguren transforms into a skiing and snowboarding destination, while in summer, it becomes a hub for hiking and mountain biking.

Cost: The gondola ride costs around **NOK 200-250** per adult for a one-way trip, and **NOK 300-350** for a round-trip ticket.

Outdoor Adventure and Extreme Sports Voss is known as the adventure capital of Norway, attracting thrill-seekers from all over the world. The town is famous for its outdoor activities, including skydiving, paragliding, canyoning, and white-water rafting. Whether you're a beginner or an experienced adventurer, Voss offers activities suitable for all levels.

What to Expect:

Skydiving: Jump out of a plane and experience an adrenaline rush while taking in breathtaking views of the fjord landscape.

Paragliding: Soar through the air and get a bird's eye view of the surrounding mountains and lakes.

Canyoning: Explore hidden canyons, navigate waterfalls, and experience Norway's rugged terrain up close.

Rafting: Test your skills on the fast-moving waters of the rivers surrounding Voss.

Cost: Prices for adventure activities vary. Expect to pay around **NOK 1,500-2,500** for activities like skydiving or paragliding, while canyoning and rafting tours may cost around **NOK 800-1,500** per person.

Voss Railway Station and Train Journey Voss is an important transport hub in the region, with its railway station being part of the **Bergen Line**, one of the most scenic train routes in the world. Traveling to or from Voss by train offers incredible views of the Norwegian countryside, making it a memorable experience in itself.

What to Expect:

Enjoy a scenic train journey to or from Bergen, which takes you through lush forests, dramatic valleys, and stunning fjord landscapes.

The journey from Bergen to Voss takes around 1.5 to 2 hours, providing plenty of time to take in the breathtaking views.

Cost: A one-way train ticket from Bergen to Voss typically costs around **NOK 150-250**, depending on the time of booking and class of travel.

Voss Church (Voss Kyrkje) Voss Church is a charming medieval church located in the center of town. Built in the early 1300s, it is a prime example of traditional Norwegian wooden architecture. The church is a peaceful place for reflection and offers insight into the religious history of the region.

What to Expect:

Visit the interior to admire the beautiful wooden carvings, stained-glass windows, and the historic altar.

Take a moment to enjoy the calm and serene atmosphere of the church, which has been an important spiritual hub for the local community for centuries.

Cost: Entry to Voss Church is free, though donations are appreciated.

Voss Museum The **Voss Museum** is dedicated to the local history, culture, and traditions of the area. It offers a fascinating look at the region's past, from its farming history to its connection with tourism and outdoor sports.

What to Expect:

Explore exhibits showcasing traditional Norwegian farming practices, local handicrafts, and historical artifacts.

Learn about the history of Voss as a travel and adventure destination and its role in the development of Norwegian tourism.

Cost: Entry to the Voss Museum costs around **NOK 100-150** per adult, with discounts for children and seniors.

What to Expect in Voss
- **Natural Beauty**: Voss is surrounded by awe-inspiring landscapes, including mountains, fjords, rivers, and forests. Whether you're hiking, rafting, or simply enjoying a boat tour, you'll be treated to some of Norway's most beautiful natural settings.
- **Adventure**: Voss is renowned for its adventure tourism, offering a wide range of outdoor activities that attract thrill-seekers from around the world. Whether it's paragliding, skydiving, or canyoning, Voss is a place where you can challenge yourself and experience the rush of adrenaline.

- **Charming Town Atmosphere**: Despite being a hub for adventure sports, Voss maintains a charming small-town atmosphere. The town center is home to quaint cafés, shops, and historical sites, providing a relaxing contrast to the high-energy outdoor activities.
- **Weather**: Voss experiences a temperate climate, with cool summers and cold winters. Be prepared for rain, especially during the fall and spring months, and dress in layers to stay comfortable in the changing weather conditions.

How to Get There

By Car: Voss is easily accessible by car from Bergen, a journey that takes around **1.5 to 2 hours** via the E16 road. The drive is scenic, offering beautiful views of the Norwegian countryside.

> **Tip**: The roads are well-maintained, but if you're driving in the winter, make sure to check weather and road conditions before traveling.

By Train: Voss is served by the **Bergen Line**, one of Norway's most scenic train routes. You can take the train from **Bergen** to **Voss**, which takes about **1.5 to 2 hours** and offers stunning views of mountains, valleys, and lakes.

By Bus: Voss is also accessible by bus from Bergen and other nearby towns. Buses provide a comfortable and affordable way to get to Voss, with a travel time of around **2-2.5 hours**.

Cost of Visiting Voss

- **Accommodation**: Prices for accommodation in Voss range from **NOK 600-1,200** per night for a mid-range hotel or guesthouse. Budget-friendly options such as hostels and campsites are available for around **NOK 300-500** per night.
- **Dining**: Dining in Voss is reasonably priced. Expect to pay around **NOK 150-250** for a meal at a local café or restaurant. More upscale dining experiences may cost **NOK 300-500** per person.
- **Activities**: Adventure activities such as skydiving, paragliding, rafting, and canyoning cost between **NOK 800-2,500** depending on the activity. Gondola rides to Mount Hanguren cost around **NOK 200-350** per person.

Tips for Visiting Voss

Seasonal Considerations: Summer (June to August) is the best time for hiking, outdoor activities, and exploring Voss, while winter (December to February) is ideal for skiing and snowboarding.

Be Prepared for Adventure: If you plan to engage in outdoor adventure activities, make sure you're physically prepared and book your tours in advance, especially during peak seasons.

Local Specialties: Be sure to try some local Norwegian dishes, such as **rakfisk** (fermented fish), **rømmegrøt** (sour cream porridge), and **kjøttkaker** (meatballs).

Voss is a unique destination that combines outdoor adventure with stunning natural beauty. Whether you're exploring the serene landscapes of the fjord, taking part in extreme sports, or

simply enjoying the small-town atmosphere, Voss offers something for everyone. With its charming surroundings and exciting activities, Voss is a must-visit destination for anyone looking to experience the best of Norwegian nature and adventure.

Scenic railways: Bergen to Oslo

One of the most remarkable ways to travel between Bergen and Oslo is by train. The **Bergen Line** (Bergensbanen), one of the world's most scenic railway routes, offers a journey that spans over **300 kilometers (186 miles)** of stunning Norwegian landscapes. The train ride between Bergen and Oslo not only connects two of Norway's major cities but also provides a chance to experience some of the most breathtaking natural scenery the country has to offer. From lush forests and deep fjords to snow-capped mountains and remote valleys, this journey is a bucket-list experience for travelers looking to discover Norway's beauty at a leisurely pace.

What to Expect on the Bergen to Oslo Train Journey

Breathtaking Landscapes
The train journey between Bergen and Oslo takes you through a series of diverse landscapes that reflect the beauty of Norway's varied terrain. Expect to see:

- **Mountain Peaks**: The train travels through the **Hardangervidda Plateau**, the largest mountain plateau in Europe. At over **1,200 meters (3,937 feet)** above sea level, this section of the journey offers spectacular views of jagged peaks and vast, open landscapes.
- **Deep Valleys and Rivers**: As you descend toward Oslo, the train passes through lush valleys, crossing over rivers that carve their way through the mountains.
- **Lakes and Fjords**: The route also passes by lakes like **Krøderen Lake** and fjords, which reflect the surrounding scenery, making for picturesque views at every turn.
- **Forests and Rolling Hills**: As the train nears Oslo, travelers will see the change in terrain, with dense forests and rolling hills offering a contrast to the more rugged mountainous landscapes seen earlier in the journey.

Comfortable and Scenic Train Ride
The train itself is a modern and comfortable way to travel. The **Vy** (formerly NSB) trains that operate this route are equipped with cozy seating, panoramic windows, and facilities like free Wi-Fi, power outlets, and restrooms.

- **Seating**: Seats are comfortable, with both standard and first-class options. First-class offers extra legroom and larger windows for enhanced viewing comfort.
- **Panoramic Windows**: One of the highlights of the journey is the panoramic windows that provide uninterrupted views of the Norwegian landscape, especially on the higher altitudes of the route.
- **Catering**: There are dining cars on board where you can enjoy light snacks, hot meals, and beverages. For a more local experience, try traditional Norwegian dishes like **smørbrød** (open-faced sandwiches) or **koldtbord** (cold cuts).

The Highest Point on the Bergen Line
The train travels through **Finse**, the highest station on the Bergen Line, situated at **1,222 meters (4,009 feet)** above sea level. Here, the landscapes are strikingly different, especially in winter when snow blankets the mountains. Finse is also a popular spot for hikers, cross-country skiers, and mountaineers.

- **What to Expect**: If traveling in winter, you'll see snow-covered mountains that resemble a winter wonderland. In summer, the greenery and crystal-clear lakes surrounding Finse are a refreshing sight.
- **Cost**: While there is no specific cost to stop at Finse, many passengers opt for the journey from Bergen to Oslo without disembarking. If you decide to make a stop here, additional time and accommodation expenses should be considered.

Oslo and Bergen – Contrasting Cities
The journey not only gives you a view of Norway's natural beauty but also highlights the contrasts between the two cities.

- **Bergen**: Known as the gateway to the fjords, Bergen is steeped in maritime history, with cobbled streets, UNESCO-listed sites like **Bryggen Wharf**, and easy access to nearby fjords.

- **Oslo**: As Norway's capital, Oslo is a bustling urban hub, known for its world-class museums, modern architecture, and vibrant cultural scene. The journey between these two cities gives a sense of the balance Norway maintains between nature and modernity.

What to Expect When Traveling Between Bergen and Oslo
Time Duration
The train journey between Bergen and Oslo takes around **6.5 to 7 hours**. The duration varies slightly depending on whether you're taking an express or slower service. The scenic views make the long journey feel shorter, as you're continually presented with new and beautiful landscapes.

Train Schedule

- Trains between Bergen and Oslo run regularly throughout the day, but departures are more frequent during peak seasons (summer and winter). The route is operated by **Vy**, Norway's national rail operator.
- In the summer months, you may also find trains offering **special scenic routes** or guided commentary about the sights you're passing.

Seasonal Views

- **Winter (December to February)**: If you're traveling during winter, expect snow-covered landscapes, especially at higher altitudes like **Finse**. The train journey offers a cozy and scenic experience while you watch the snow-dusted mountains pass by.
- **Spring (March to May)**: Spring brings fresh greenery, blooming flowers, and milder temperatures. It's the perfect season for witnessing the transition from snowy peaks to lush valleys.
- **Summer (June to August)**: Summer is the most popular season for tourists, offering lush green valleys, clear blue skies, and long daylight hours.
- **Autumn (September to November)**: Fall provides a stunning display of autumn colors, with the forested regions showing off vibrant shades of orange, red, and yellow.

How to Get on the Train
Starting Point: Bergen Station
Bergen Station, or **Bergen Sentralstasjon**, is located in the city center and is easily accessible by public transportation, including buses and taxis. The station has a range of services and facilities, including shops, cafes, and waiting areas.

Arrival Point: Oslo Central Station
Oslo S (Sentralstasjon) is the main railway station in Oslo and is centrally located, making it easy to connect to other modes of transport. The station is connected to the metro, buses, and trams, allowing you to seamlessly continue your journey from Oslo to other parts of the city.

Booking Tickets

- Tickets can be purchased online through **Vy**'s website or app, at ticket machines, or at the ticket counter in the stations. It is advisable to book in advance, especially during peak seasons, to guarantee your seat.
- You can choose between standard and first-class tickets, with first-class offering additional comfort and services.

Cost:

- A one-way ticket for a standard class train journey between Bergen and Oslo generally costs around **NOK 399-899** depending on the time of booking, class, and season. First-class tickets typically cost between **NOK 600-1,200**.
- Discounts may be available for children, seniors, or those booking early.

Tips for the Train Journey

- **Book in Advance**: Especially during high tourist seasons (summer and winter holidays), it's a good idea to book your tickets well in advance, as trains can fill up quickly.

- **Bring a Camera**: The scenery is spectacular, so having a camera or smartphone ready to capture the breathtaking views is essential.

- **Layer Your Clothing**: Weather conditions can vary greatly, especially if traveling through the higher altitudes. Bring layers to stay comfortable, and don't forget a warm jacket if traveling in winter.

- **Take Advantage of the Panoramic Windows**: The train features large windows that allow you to enjoy uninterrupted views. Be sure to sit on the side of the train that offers the best vantage points.

The **Bergen to Oslo train journey** is more than just a means of transport—it's a stunning showcase of Norway's natural beauty. Whether you're traveling for leisure or to connect with another destination, this scenic route offers an unforgettable experience. From the wild, snow-covered landscapes of the mountains to the tranquil beauty of Norwegian lakes and forests, the Bergen Line is an iconic way to explore the heart of Norway.

Chapter 10. Insider Tips and Travel Hacks

Packing for Norwegian weather

Packing for Norwegian Weather: A Comprehensive Guide

Norway's weather can be unpredictable and often varies significantly depending on the season and region. Whether you're visiting the coastal areas of Bergen or the mountainous terrains of the fjords, it's crucial to be prepared for all weather conditions. Packing for Norway requires planning for a range of temperatures, unexpected rain, and varying climates depending on whether you're in the cities or the wilderness.

Understanding Norwegian Weather

Before packing, it's important to understand Norway's weather patterns:

- **Coastal Areas (Bergen, Stavanger, Tromsø)**: Coastal areas, especially in the west, tend to have milder, wetter weather due to the influence of the Gulf Stream. Expect frequent rain and temperatures that hover around **10°C to 15°C** (50°F to 59°F) in the summer and **-5°C to 5°C** (23°F to 41°F) in the winter.
- **Mountainous Areas (Hiking Trails, Hardangervidda, Jotunheimen)**: The mountains have more extreme conditions, with temperatures dropping considerably even in summer months. Expect chilly temperatures, even in the warmer months, and snow that can last well into spring at higher elevations.
- **Northern Norway (Tromsø, Lofoten)**: In the north, temperatures can be cold even in summer, with a chance of snow and freezing temperatures in winter. Coastal regions experience milder winters compared to the inland areas, but the weather can be quite variable.

Clothing Essentials for All Seasons

Regardless of the time of year, layering is key when it comes to Norwegian weather. The country's climate demands clothing that can handle both extreme cold and unexpected warmth.

Base Layers

- **Thermal Underwear**: Lightweight, moisture-wicking thermal undergarments are crucial for both winter and summer, especially for outdoor activities like hiking. Wool or merino wool is excellent as it keeps you warm even when wet and is breathable.
- **Moisture-Wicking Tops and Bottoms**: For a base layer, choose clothing made of merino wool or synthetic fibers like polyester. These fabrics wick moisture away from your skin, keeping you dry and warm.

Mid-Layer

- **Fleece Jackets or Sweaters**: A mid-layer is important for providing extra insulation. A fleece jacket or sweater offers warmth without adding too much bulk, making it perfect for layering.
- **Light Insulated Jackets**: For cooler days in the summer or winter, a lightweight insulated jacket can add an extra layer of warmth when needed.

Outer Layer

- **Waterproof Jacket and Pants**: Norway experiences frequent rain, particularly in coastal areas like Bergen, so a good-quality waterproof jacket and pants are a must. Opt for a breathable, windproof material to keep you dry during sudden showers while avoiding overheating.
- **Windproof Layer**: Even in the summer, strong winds can make the temperature feel colder, so a lightweight windproof jacket is beneficial.

- **Down or Insulated Coat**: For winter or colder weather, pack a warm, insulated down coat to stay cozy. For hiking or outdoor activities, make sure it is breathable to avoid sweating.

Accessories

- **Warm Hat and Gloves**: Even in the summer, temperatures can drop significantly in the evenings, especially in the mountains. A wool hat and gloves will keep you warm, and gloves with touchscreen tips can be handy for your phone or camera.
- **Scarf or Neck Gaiter**: A scarf or neck gaiter will protect you from wind and cold, particularly in the northern and mountain regions.
- **Sunglasses and Sunscreen**: Norway is known for its beautiful landscapes, so bring sunglasses to protect your eyes from the bright sunlight. Sunscreen is also essential, as even the cool summer air can burn your skin under the strong Scandinavian sun, particularly in the north during the midnight sun.
- **Rain Poncho or Packable Waterproof Gear**: A lightweight rain poncho can serve as an emergency waterproof option when hiking or exploring.

Footwear

- **Waterproof Hiking Boots**: A pair of sturdy, waterproof boots is essential for trekking through Norwegian nature, particularly in rainy or snowy conditions. Choose boots with good ankle support and durable soles for rough trails.
- **Casual Shoes or Sneakers**: For urban exploration or non-hiking activities, a comfortable pair of sneakers or casual shoes is a must.
- **Thermal Socks**: Invest in moisture-wicking, insulating socks (preferably wool) for warmth and dryness. Bring extra pairs for long hikes or multiple days of outdoor activities.

Seasonal Packing Considerations

The weather will vary depending on the time of year, so it's important to adjust your packing list accordingly.

Summer (June to August)

While summer in Norway can bring pleasant weather, it's still important to be prepared for cooler temperatures, particularly in the evenings or in the mountains.

- **Light Layers**: You'll need light clothing such as T-shirts, long-sleeve shirts, and pants, but still bring along a jacket or sweater for cooler days.
- **Rain Protection**: Always pack a waterproof jacket and a pair of rainproof pants, as summer is still rainy in many parts of the country.
- **Swimwear**: In summer, Norway's fjords and lakes offer opportunities for swimming. Bring a swimsuit if you plan to swim in the cold waters.
- **Sun Protection**: Sunscreen and sunglasses are essential, especially in the northern regions where the sun never sets during the summer months.

Autumn (September to November)

Autumn is marked by cooler temperatures and changing weather conditions, so prepare for both warmth and chilly winds.

- **Layering Is Key**: Start with base layers, a mid-layer for warmth, and an insulated outer jacket for unpredictable weather.
- **Boots for Wet Weather**: Fall can be quite wet, so waterproof boots are a necessity, especially for hiking in the fjords or walking through forests covered in fallen leaves.

- **Rain Gear**: A good rain jacket and waterproof pants are recommended for dealing with autumn showers.

Winter (December to February)

Norwegian winters can be harsh, especially in the northern regions and mountain areas. It's essential to stay warm and dry.

- **Heavy Insulated Layers**: A down jacket or parka is a must to stay warm. Underneath, wear thermal base layers and fleece for insulation.
- **Thermal and Wool Accessories**: Wool hats, gloves, and scarves will keep you comfortable during outdoor activities in the cold weather.
- **Winter Boots**: Insulated, waterproof boots with good traction are necessary to handle icy conditions.
- **Ski Gear**: If you're planning on skiing or snowboarding, bring your own gear or rent it locally in ski resorts.

Spring (March to May)

Spring is unpredictable, with a mix of snow and rain. Temperatures range from chilly to mild, so dressing in layers is key.

- **Layered Clothing**: Start with a light base layer, and add an insulating mid-layer like a fleece. A waterproof jacket is essential to protect from both rain and snow.
- **Waterproof Footwear**: Waterproof boots or shoes are ideal as the snow begins to melt and the ground becomes wet.
- **Light Gloves and Hat**: Bring a lighter hat and gloves that can be easily packed away when not needed.

Packing Tips

- **Pack Light:** Due to the varying weather conditions, you'll need versatile clothing that can be layered. Avoid packing too many heavy items, as you'll want flexibility in your layers.
- **Waterproof Everything**: Whether it's your shoes, jacket, or backpack, water resistance is key to staying dry during your travels.
- **Bring an Extra Bag**: A small waterproof daypack is great for day trips, especially when hiking or taking part in outdoor activities. Keep your electronics and valuables safe from rain.
- **Check Weather Forecasts**: Before your trip, always check the weather forecast for the specific regions you'll be visiting, especially if you're heading to remote locations or planning activities like hiking in the mountains.

Packing for Norwegian weather is all about being prepared for a range of conditions. The key to a comfortable trip is layering your clothing, ensuring you have the right waterproof gear, and being ready for rapid weather changes, especially if you plan to explore the outdoors. With this comprehensive packing guide, you'll be ready to enjoy everything Norway has to offer, from the bustling cities to the serene fjords and majestic mountains.

Avoiding tourist traps

Bergen, with its rich history, scenic fjords, and charming streets, draws visitors from all over the world. However, like many popular tourist destinations, it has its share of tourist traps—places or activities that may seem appealing at first but can be overpriced, overcrowded, or lack authenticity. To make the most of your visit and truly experience the magic of Bergen, it's essential to navigate around these traps and explore the city in a more genuine, local way.

Steer Clear of Overpriced Souvenir Shops in Bryggen

Bergen's Bryggen Wharf is a UNESCO World Heritage site and a must-see for any visitor. While its historic buildings and picturesque views are a highlight, the souvenir shops lining the streets are often filled with overpriced trinkets, ranging from mass-produced Viking helmets to cheap jewelry.

How to avoid it:

- **Seek out local markets**: Instead of buying souvenirs from shops in Bryggen, head to the local markets or smaller, independent shops scattered throughout the city. Places like the **Fish Market (Fisketorget)** and **Torgallmenningen** often feature artisanal products and crafts that are more unique and locally made.
- **Focus on quality**: Look for handmade goods, such as Norwegian knitwear, locally produced chocolates, and artisan items that reflect Bergen's culture rather than generic souvenirs.

Skip the High-Cost Fløibanen Funicular for a Scenic Hike
The Fløibanen Funicular, which takes visitors up to the top of Mount Fløyen, is one of Bergen's most popular attractions. While it offers stunning views, the ticket prices can be quite steep, especially for a short ride.

How to avoid it:

- **Hike to the top**: If you're up for a little adventure and want to enjoy the scenery more intimately, hike to the top of **Mount Fløyen** instead. The trail is relatively easy and offers a more authentic experience, allowing you to take in the lush forest, quiet paths, and panoramic views at your own pace.
- **Free viewpoints**: For a great view of the city without the need to pay for the funicular, take a walk up to **Mount Ulriken** or explore some of the other lesser-known viewpoints around the city.

Avoid Overcrowded Boat Tours and Choose More Intimate Fjord Experiences
Norway's fjords are undoubtedly one of its biggest attractions, and many boat tours operate in Bergen, offering scenic cruises through the beautiful landscapes. However, many of these tours can be overcrowded, expensive, and tourist-centric, often taking you to the same popular spots filled with large groups of people.

How to avoid it:

- **Opt for smaller tours**: Look for **private or small-group boat tours** that provide a more intimate experience of the fjords. Many local operators offer personalized tours to hidden gems that larger tours miss. Some even provide opportunities for **kayaking or small boat adventures** to get closer to the natural beauty of the fjords.
- **Explore beyond the standard tours**: If you're keen to visit the famous fjords, consider exploring less popular ones like **Hardangerfjord** or **Sognefjord** to escape the crowds and see more serene landscapes.

Don't Fall for Overhyped "Norwegian Cultural Shows"
Bergen is rich in culture and history, and while many tour operators offer "traditional Norwegian cultural shows," many of these performances are designed more for tourists than for authentic cultural immersion. These shows often present a commercialized version of Norwegian folklore and music, with high prices that don't justify the experience.

How to avoid it:

- **Seek local events**: Instead of the touristy shows, check out **local theaters** or **music festivals** where you can enjoy genuine Norwegian performances. Events like the **Bergen International Festival** offer a mix of local culture, music, and arts that are much more immersive.

- **Explore museums**: Bergen has numerous museums that showcase authentic Norwegian history and culture, such as the **KODE Art Museums**, where you can experience local art and heritage away from the touristy hustle.

Avoid the Mainstream Restaurants in Tourist Hotspots
Bergen's dining scene is fantastic, but many of the restaurants in high-traffic tourist areas (like near Bryggen and the Fish Market) cater primarily to tourists. These restaurants can offer subpar food at inflated prices, often serving generic, mass-produced dishes that don't capture the true flavors of Bergen's cuisine.

How to avoid it:

- **Eat where locals eat**: To get a real taste of Norwegian cuisine, head to the neighborhoods where the locals eat, like **Sandviken** or **Nygårdsparken**. You'll find more authentic restaurants serving fresh, locally sourced food at better prices.
- **Try local specialties**: Look for places offering **Norwegian seafood** dishes, such as **klippfisk** (dried cod) or **rakfisk** (fermented fish), or visit **small, family-run eateries** that take pride in using fresh ingredients.
- **Explore food markets**: The **Fish Market** is a great place to try fresh seafood in a more casual, authentic setting. Here, you can sample fish straight off the boat, prepared fresh by local vendors.

Avoid Taking the Main Tourist Bus Routes
Many visitors to Bergen opt for organized bus tours that hit all the well-known landmarks in the city. While these tours can provide some useful information, they often cater to the lowest common denominator and can be both impersonal and time-consuming.

How to avoid it:

- **Go for self-guided tours**: Bergen's compact size and walkability make it easy to explore on foot. Opt for **self-guided walking tours** to discover the city at your own pace. You can use apps or local guides to get information on the city's history and landmarks.
- **Rent a bike**: Bergen is a bike-friendly city, and renting a bike allows you to explore more freely and discover hidden spots that are off the beaten path.

Don't Overpay for City Viewpoints
While Bergen offers some stunning viewpoints, many of the best spots can be accessed for free or with minimal effort. Instead of paying for a ticket to a popular viewpoint like **Mount Fløyen** or **Ulriken**, consider hiking or exploring less crowded locations.

How to avoid it:

- **Free viewpoints**: Explore **Kopervik Hill** or **Bergenhus Fortress** for panoramic views of the city, which are both free and less crowded.
- **Take the scenic route**: Whether on foot or by bike, the trails leading to various viewpoints are often free and allow you to enjoy nature without the crowds.

Bergen is a city brimming with culture, history, and natural beauty, and by avoiding tourist traps, you can experience it in a more authentic and affordable way. Instead of following the crowds to overpriced attractions, seek out the local gems, explore lesser-known hiking trails, dine where the locals do, and immerse yourself in the true essence of the city. With this guide, you'll be well-equipped to uncover the hidden treasures of Bergen and make your trip one to remember for all the right reasons.

Budgeting your trip

Bergen, Norway, is undoubtedly a dream destination, with its stunning fjords, rich history, and vibrant culture. However, like many popular travel spots, it can be expensive if you don't plan ahead. Whether you're traveling on a shoestring budget or looking for ways to save money without compromising on the experience, there are plenty of strategies to help you manage costs while still enjoying the best that Bergen has to offer.

Airfare and Transportation: Finding Affordable Flights and Getting Around

Airfare:

- **Book in advance**: Flights to Bergen can vary greatly depending on the time of year, so it's essential to book your tickets well in advance. Keep an eye on deals from low-cost carriers such as **Norwegian Air** or **SAS** for more affordable options.
- **Off-peak flights**: To secure the best prices, aim to fly during the off-peak months (late fall to early spring) when demand is lower. Avoid the summer months, as this is peak tourist season.
- **Consider nearby airports**: If flights into Bergen are too expensive, consider flying into **Oslo** and taking the scenic **Bergen Railway** to the city. This can offer great views of the Norwegian countryside and sometimes costs less.

Getting around Bergen:

- **Public transportation**: Bergen has an efficient public transportation system, including buses, trams, and ferries. A **Bergen Card** offers unlimited travel on all public transport and discounted entry to many attractions.
    - **Cost**: The Bergen Card costs about **NOK 485** for 24 hours, **NOK 630** for 48 hours, and **NOK 755** for 72 hours.
- **Biking**: Bergen is a bike-friendly city, and renting a bike can be an economical and fun way to explore. Several bike rental shops offer daily rates.
- **Walking**: Bergen is a small city, and many of its attractions are within walking distance from one another. Exploring on foot not only saves money but also gives you the chance to experience the city more intimately.

Accommodation: Finding Budget-Friendly Stays
Accommodation is often one of the largest expenses for travelers, but there are numerous options in Bergen that fit a variety of budgets.

Budget-friendly stays:

- **Hostels**: Bergen has several hostels that offer affordable rates. **Marken Gjestehus** and **Bergen Hostel Montana** are both excellent options for those looking to save money on accommodation.
- **Cost**: Dormitory beds typically range from **NOK 250–400** per night, and private rooms can cost around **NOK 600–1,000** per night.
- **Budget hotels**: There are a number of budget hotel chains, such as **Citybox Bergen** and **P-Hotels Bergen**, which offer comfortable stays without the hefty price tag.
- **Cost**: Rates for budget hotels range from **NOK 800–1,500** per night, depending on the season.
- **Airbnb**: If you prefer a more local experience, check out Airbnb listings for apartments, rooms, or even cozy cabins outside the city center. You can often find more affordable options this way, especially if you're traveling with a group.
- **Cost**: Prices for Airbnb in Bergen start from around **NOK 500** per night for a private room, while entire apartments can be found for **NOK 1,000–2,500**.

Dining: Eating on a Budget

Norwegian food can be expensive, especially when dining out at tourist hotspots. However, there are plenty of ways to enjoy Bergen's culinary delights without blowing your budget.

Affordable dining options:

- **Local eateries and cafés**: Opt for local, family-owned cafés and eateries where you can enjoy traditional Norwegian food at lower prices. **Kaffemisjonen**, for example, offers reasonably priced coffee and sandwiches, while **Pingvinen** is a casual pub serving hearty Norwegian fare.
- **Cost**: Meals at local cafés and smaller restaurants typically range from **NOK 100–250** per person.
- **Bergen Fish Market**: While some stalls in the Fish Market may be expensive, there are also more affordable options for fresh seafood. Opt for smaller portions or street food-style seafood like fish cakes or shrimp sandwiches.
- **Cost**: Expect to pay around **NOK 100–200** for a simple seafood meal.
- **Self-catering**: If you want to save money, consider buying fresh ingredients from local markets or grocery stores and cooking your own meals. **Rema 1000** and **Coop** are popular grocery chains in Norway, offering a wide range of affordable options.
- **Cost**: A basic grocery shop for two people can cost around **NOK 300–500** for a few meals.

Attractions and Activities: Exploring on a Budget

Bergen is home to numerous free or low-cost activities and attractions that allow you to explore the city without breaking the bank.

Free and affordable attractions:

- **Bryggen Wharf**: Wander through the historic wooden buildings of Bryggen, which are free to explore. It's a UNESCO World Heritage site and an essential part of Bergen's history.
- **Mount Fløyen and hiking trails**: While the Fløibanen funicular has a fee, you can also hike up to **Mount Fløyen** for free. The trail offers fantastic views of the city, fjords, and surrounding landscapes.
- **KODE Art Museums**: While some museums charge an entrance fee, many offer discounted or free admission on certain days. Check for **special offers** and events before you go.
- **Cost**: Admission to museums like KODE can range from **NOK 50–150**.
- **Fjord Cruises**: While some fjord tours can be pricey, there are more affordable options like **self-guided boat tours** or smaller, local companies offering budget cruises.

Shopping: Saving While Shopping for Souvenirs
Shopping in Bergen can be expensive, especially in tourist-heavy areas like Bryggen. However, there are ways to find unique souvenirs without overspending.

Budget shopping tips:

- **Street markets**: Visit local street markets such as the **Fish Market** and **Hanseatic Square** for handmade crafts, Norwegian wool items, and local delicacies at reasonable prices.
- **Discount stores**: Consider shopping at **Norwegian discount stores** like **Europris** or **Kiwi**, where you can find affordable goods, from souvenirs to local products.

Money-Saving Tips for Your Trip to Bergen

- **Plan for tipping**: In Norway, tipping is not mandatory, and service charges are typically included in bills. However, rounding up the bill or leaving a small tip for exceptional service is appreciated.
- **Cash vs. card**: Norway is a cashless society, and most places accept credit or debit cards. It's wise to avoid carrying large amounts of cash, as you might face additional fees for foreign exchange.
- **Currency exchange**: Avoid exchanging money at airports or tourist hotspots, where the rates are often less favorable. Use ATMs or exchange offices in the city for better rates.

- **Stay flexible**: Keep an eye out for last-minute deals and special offers on tours, accommodation, and activities. Many companies offer discounts for booking in advance, or during low-demand periods.

Bergen offers something for every type of traveler, whether you're splurging on luxury or looking to explore on a budget. By planning ahead, choosing the right accommodation, dining smartly, and taking advantage of free and affordable attractions, you can experience all that this charming city has to offer without straining your wallet. With these budgeting tips, you'll be able to enjoy Bergen's stunning fjords, rich culture, and history, making the most of your trip while keeping costs under control.

Chapter 11. Closing Thoughts

Encouragement for your journey

As you embark on your journey to Bergen, remember that this city, nestled between the dramatic Norwegian fjords and surrounded by rolling hills, has much to offer. From its rich history to breathtaking landscapes, every step you take will lead you to experiences that will stay with you for a lifetime.

The winding streets of Bryggen, the serene calm of the fjords, and the panoramic views from Mount Ulriken are waiting for you to discover them. With every hike, every local delicacy you try, and every moment spent immersed in nature, you'll connect more deeply with the essence of Bergen. It's a place where adventure meets culture, and history meets nature, offering you endless opportunities to make lasting memories.

Don't let the challenges of budgeting or planning stand in your way—Bergen is a city that rewards curiosity and exploration. Every corner of the city holds something new, something unexpected. Whether it's a quaint café, a hidden art gallery, or an unforgettable view of the fjords, the experiences you seek are right at your fingertips.

So, go ahead—take the plunge and immerse yourself in everything Bergen has to offer. This journey is not just about ticking off attractions from a list; it's about soaking in the atmosphere, embracing the beauty, and finding joy in the moments of discovery. You've made the right choice by picking up this guide, and I'm confident that your time in Bergen will be everything you hoped for and more.

Thank you for trusting this guide as part of your adventure. May your time in Bergen be filled with unforgettable moments, new friendships, and a sense of wonder that will stay with you long after your journey comes to an end. Safe travels, and remember—the best part of the adventure is just getting started!

Bonus

Importance of the Bonus: Simple Common Phrases to Help You Interact Like a Local

This bonus section is designed to enhance your experience in Bergen by helping you connect with locals in a meaningful way. Learning a few simple, common phrases in Norwegian can make your travels more enjoyable and authentic. Whether it's ordering food, asking for directions, or striking up a conversation, knowing these phrases will help you navigate the city with confidence and show respect for the local culture. It's a small effort that will go a long way in making your journey smoother and more enriching, allowing you to engage with Bergen's vibrant community in a more personal way.

Common phrases

- **Hello / Hi**
  Hei
  (Pronounced: "Hi")
- **Good morning**
  God morgen
  (Pronounced: "Good mohr-en")
- **Good evening**
  God kveld
  (Pronounced: "Good kvel-d")
- **How are you?**
  Hvordan har du det?
  (Pronounced: "Vor-dahn har doo deh?")

- **I'm fine, thank you.**
  Jeg har det bra, takk.
  (Pronounced: "Yay har deh bra, tahk")
- **Please**
  Vær så snill
  (Pronounced: "Vahr soh snill")
- **Thank you**
  Takk
  (Pronounced: "Tahk")
- **Excuse me**
  Unnskyld meg
  (Pronounced: "Oon-shild my")
- **Yes**
  Ja
  (Pronounced: "Yah")
- **No**
  Nei
  (Pronounced: "Nay")
- **Where is...?**
  Hvor er...?
  (Pronounced: "Vor air")
- **How much does this cost?**
  Hvor mye koster dette?
  (Pronounced: "Vor mee-eh kohs-ter deh-teh?")
- **Can you help me?**
  Kan du hjelpe meg?
  (Pronounced: "Kahn doo yel-peh my")
- **I don't understand.**
  Jeg forstår ikke.
  (Pronounced: "Yay for-stor eek-keh")
- **Goodbye**
  Ha det bra
  (Pronounced: "Hah deh bra")

Tourism Websites

- **Visit Bergen**
  Website: https://www.visitbergen.com
  A comprehensive guide to Bergen, with information on attractions, events, tours, and accommodations.

- **Visit Norway**
  Website: https://www.visitnorway.com
  The official tourism site for Norway, offering detailed information about Bergen and other destinations.

- **Bergen Tourist Information**
  Website: https://www.bergen-guide.com
  Provides essential travel information and services in Bergen.

Transportation and Travel

- **Bergen Airport (Flesland)**
  Website: https://www.flesland.no/en
  For flight schedules, airport services, and transport options to and from Bergen.

- **Vy (Train Travel in Norway)**
  Website: https://www.vy.no/en
  Information on trains from Bergen to other cities, including the scenic Bergen-Oslo railway.

- **Skyss (Public Transport in Bergen)**
  Website: https://www.skyss.no/en/
  For schedules and routes for buses and light rail in Bergen.

- **Bergen Taxis**
  Website: https://www.taxibergen.no
  For booking a taxi in Bergen.

Local Services

- **Bergen Aquarium**
  Website: https://www.akvariet.no/en
  Information on exhibits, activities, and opening hours for the Bergen Aquarium.

- **VilVite Science Center**
  Website: https://www.vilvite.no/en
  Offers interactive exhibits and family-friendly science activities.

- **Bergen Kunsthall**
  Website: https://www.kunsthall.no/en
  For contemporary art exhibitions and cultural events in Bergen.

Accommodation Contacts

- **Hotel Norge by Scandic**
  Website: https://www.scandichotels.com
  Booking information for one of Bergen's luxury hotels.

- **Citybox Bergen**
  Website: https://www.citybox.no/en/bergen/
  Budget-friendly accommodation in Bergen.

- **Airbnb Bergen**
  Website: https://www.airbnb.com/bergen-norway
  For alternative accommodation options, such as private apartments or homes.

Fjord Tours

- **Norway in a Nutshell**
  Website: https://www.norwaynutshell.com
  A site that offers various fjord tours from Bergen, including train, bus, and boat combinations.

- **Fjord Tours**
  Website: https://www.fjordtours.com
  Offering guided tours to explore Norway's stunning fjords.

Emergency Contacts

- **Emergency Services** (Police, Fire, Ambulance)
  Phone: **112**
  For any emergency in Bergen and across Norway.

- **Bergen Tourist Information**
  Phone: **+47 55 55 20 00**
  For general inquiries about Bergen and its attractions.

Travel Journal

Date	Destination/Stop	Key Activities/Excursions	Memorable Moments	Food Tried/Restaurants	Thoughts & Reflections	Photos Taken (Yes/No)
Day 1						
Day 2						
Day 3						
Day 4						
Day 5						
Day 6						
Day 7						
Packing List:		Special Memories to Remember:			Important Contacts/Information	

Dear Reader,

Thank you for choosing this travel guide as your companion to Bergen, Norway. It means the world to me that you've trusted this book to help shape your journey and experiences in this magical destination.

Every page you've read, every tip you've discovered, and every piece of advice shared here has been crafted with immense care, dedication, and love for travel. To create this guide, I invested countless hours of research, significant resources, and even ventured to Bergen myself to ensure I could deliver the most accurate, insightful, and inspiring recommendations. This wasn't just a book for me—it was a labor of passion to help you experience the wonders of Bergen in the best way possible.

Your feedback and reviews hold extraordinary value to me, not just as a writer but as someone striving to create meaningful and helpful resources for travelers like you. A positive review from you is not just a few words; it's an acknowledgment of my efforts, a boost to my progress as a travel guide writer, and a light that helps guide my future work.

If this guide has helped you plan your trip, made your journey smoother, or added a little extra magic to your adventure, I kindly ask for a moment of your time to leave a review. Your kind words and thoughtful feedback will encourage others to explore Bergen while supporting me in continuing to provide guides that inspire meaningful travel.

Thank you again for being part of this journey. I hope Bergen leaves you with memories to cherish for a lifetime, and I can't wait to accompany you on your next adventure!

Warm regards,
Libby Martinez

Printed in Dunstable, United Kingdom